Out of the Woods

Zickefoose

OUT
OF THE
WOODS

A Bird Watcher's Year

Ora E. Anderson

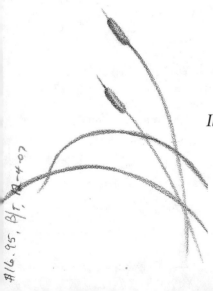

Edited by Deborah Griffith

Illustrations by Julie Zickefoose

Foreword by Jean Andrews

Ohio University Press Athens
OCM 76864357

Ohio University Press, Athens, Ohio 45701

www.ohio.edu/oupress

© 2007 by Ohio University Press

Illustrations copyright © 2007 by Julie Zickefoose

Printed in the United States of America

Ohio University Press books are printed on acid-free paper ⊗ ™

15 14 13 12 11 10 09 08 07   5 4 3 2 1

"An October Walk" was published in the September/October 2001
issue of *Bird Watcher's Digest*.

Library of Congress Cataloging-in-Publication Data

Anderson, Ora E., 1911–2006.

  Out of the woods : a bird watcher's year / Ora E. Anderson ;
edited by Deborah Griffith ; illustrations by Julie Zickefoose ;
foreword by Jean Andrews.

    p. cm.

  ISBN-13: 978-0-8214-1741-6 (hardcover : alk. paper)

  ISBN-10: 0-8214-1741-X (hardcover : alk. paper)

  ISBN-13: 978-0-8214-1742-3 (pbk. : alk. paper)

  ISBN-10: 0-8214-1742-8 (pbk. : alk. paper)

  1. Bird watching—Ohio—Anecdotes. 2. Birds—Ohio—
Anecdotes. 3. Anderson, Ora E., 1911–2006. I. Griffith,
Deborah, 1954– II. Title.

  QL684.O3A53 2007

  598'.07234771—dc22

                                         2006039607

Contents

Summer

Fall

Winter

Foreword

Ora Anderson and I sit on the edge of his farm pond and talk about his trees and hills, ponds and marshes, and all the changes that have occurred on this southern Ohio landscape. The essays in this book reflect such stories as I have actually heard. On such occasions by the pond, the pleasure is enhanced by watching a muskrat glide effortlessly across the water's surface or observing a family of turtles emerge from the depths for a morsel or two of fish food tossed out to the various bass, bluegill, and bullhead catfish. This is what it's like to spend time with this self-styled "Kentucky hillbilly," when the conversation may turn to many subjects, but those that harmonize best with the changing seasons are the retelling of anecdotes from almost a century of living in or near the Appalachian Mountains.

As he tells the story, Ora "Andy" Anderson was born in a log cabin on the Mill branch of the "fur" Middle Fork of the Licking River in Magoffin County, Kentucky, about three miles from Salyersville, the county seat. In 1913, his family moved across the Ohio River to the flatlands or "the onion fields" of northwestern Ohio, near Ada, where the entire family could work on the peat moss farms, growing and harvesting onions, cabbage, and celery. En route they were stranded in Columbus by the February 1913 flood and lived for two weeks in Union Station (the railroad depot, since demolished), two weeks in a church basement, then in a small house across the Scioto River from downtown Columbus. At that point his father said, "That's enough of Ohio." The family moved back to Magoffin County, Kentucky, then two years later to Catlettsburg, Kentucky, where they remained until 1929. Anderson's formal education, as he reminds his friends, culminated with a diploma from Catlettsburg High School.

In 1929 his father bought a forty-acre farm in Jackson County, Ohio, and moved his family to the Ohio foothills of the Appalachians. They worked the land; the Great Depression was on, and life was tough. But not for a young man like Anderson, who, through persistence, got a job as the only reporter on the twice-weekly *Jackson Herald* newspaper for a salary of $6 per week. A year later he became the editor—thanks to the fact, Anderson claims, that the publisher could not afford a good, experienced editor. Anderson's salary was later raised to $29 per week. It was on one of his reporting assignments that he met and interviewed his future wife, Harriet Jacoby, an Athens County farm girl who had traveled two counties west to Jackson that summer to be the 4-H agent. Anderson often reminisces about his wife Harriet and about how, as a graduate of Ohio University and full of life, she taught him about love, good manners, the value of art and drama, frugality, ambition, and the need for a career destination.

So Anderson moved his wife and their baby daughter, Jan, to Salem, Ohio, and became editor of the *Farm and Dairy,* a weekly farm newspaper serving nine counties in northeastern Ohio. By 1941, he had become the district manager of the Dairymen's Cooperative Sales Association, a dairy farmers' marketing cooperative organization. He recalls, "I scheduled twenty-one trucks that picked up milk at each farm and delivered it to dairy company plants. I was responsible for bargaining for the monthly price of milk per hundred pounds for the farmers." Anderson represented 1,400 farmers in transporting and marketing their milk and acted as the spokesman for dairymen on matters before the Ohio legislature. It was during this time that his second daughter, Susan, was born.

In 1942 Anderson became the executive secretary to the Ohio Dairy Products Association, representing processors and distributors in all typical trade association activities, including legislation. After relocating his young family to Columbus, his main task was working the Ohio General Assembly on issues of interest to the dairy industry. Nine years later he was hired by the Ohio Bankers Association as their assistant manager. All legislative issues affecting banking both in Ohio and Washington, D.C., became his interests; he also was responsible for editing bulletins and a monthly magazine, arranging conferences and conventions, and starting short-term schools for bank employees at various Ohio schools (Ohio University, Miami, Kent State, Bowling Green). He also served for seven years as chair of the board of trustees of the short-course school of banking at the University of Wisconsin–Madison, serving banks in sixteen states. He retired as executive manager of the Ohio Bankers Association in 1972.

At the height of his bank association career, Anderson and his wife began looking for a place to which they could eventually retire. After considerable discussion and searching, they decided to return to Harriet's childhood home. They bought her family's farm in Athens County in 1956, built the first pond that year, planted trees, and built their family cottage one year later. They would slowly help convert the worn-out ninety-eight-acre farm into a true nature preserve, eventually planting thirty thousand trees, building three more ponds and marshes and two miles of trails, and maintaining open areas for wildlife and bird watching.

Anderson's lifelong interest in nature included decades of advocacy for natural areas in Ohio, and his role in shaping organizations such as The Nature Conservancy of Ohio has been well documented. His eyewitness account of the first land purchases in Appalachian Ohio that eventually became the Wayne National Forest has been made into an award-winning documentary video, *A Forest Returns.* In addition to witnessing and reporting on the beginning of Ohio's only national forest seventy years ago, Anderson remained an active participant during fifty years of public meetings regarding Wayne National Forest land management.

A longtime bird carver, poet, nature writer, and storyteller, Anderson guides his audience down a path paved with local lore and anecdotes. Through it all, he is an Appalachian—one whose sense of self is rooted in his sense of place, as experienced in the rugged and scenic foothills of the Appalachian Mountains. This is especially evident at his tree farm, the inspiration as well as the repository of his memories. To talk with Anderson is to visualize a bygone era, as he paints a vivid portrait of the past through stories and anecdotes. His seasoned perspective on matters ranging from successful lobbying to mountain remedies passed down to him by his Kentucky grandmother, Queen Victoria Green, as well as his astute observations of seasonal changes in the Ohio hill country, contribute to a deepening sense of place for all who visit or live here. As Ohio University President Emeritus Charles Ping recently said to me as he described a walk in the woods on Anderson's farm, "When you walk the land with Andy, you see things that you see *only* when he helps you to see them."

Jean Andrews

Preface

Why I Write

The word "nature" has a precise meaning to me, as it does to almost anyone who takes a moment to reflect on a passing thunderstorm, the erratic flight of a monarch butterfly, or the wrack line of an ocean beach.

"Nature," we readily agree, is in the touch of a cooling breeze on our sweating forehead in mid-July and the crunching sounds of hard-packed snow responding to our homeward steps in a January dusk.

The park in the heart of the city spells the word "nature" just as clearly as a float trip down the rapids of the Gauley River in West Virginia's mountains. It comes as no surprise, then, that the nature observations I make speak as clearly as my vocabulary and my personal experiences will allow. Furthermore, I fully expect them to stir within those who hear my words a sense of participation, or curiosity, or discovery.

John James Audubon did not see or identify every bird species in North America. Daniel Boone wasn't even interested in such trifles as prothonotary warblers when he came to Kentucky. George Catlin painted American Indians throughout the western plains and mountain valleys, but he missed the Gros Ventre, the Blackfoot, and dozens of other equally colorful tribes.

That's just the "nature" of our world. Yet to me that is the charm of everything out yonder. The encyclopedic knowledge of geology of John McPhee, the passion of the late Ed Abbey, and the ability of Stephen Jay Gould to trace the ancestry of natural history from Eden to Einstein don't diminish my own meager observations one whit, whatever a whit is.

It is certainly unimportant that a yellow-breasted chat hooked me on bird watching more than seventy long and joyful years ago. If it hadn't been that chat doing its butterfly dance over a blackberry thicket on an eastern Kentucky ridge, quite surely it would have been a flock of nighthawks, a booming grouse, or a house sparrow in our chicken yard. Some things are predestined—in "nature."

So I write of nature—the outdoors, the roll of seasons, the pain of a yellow-jacket sting, the cooling touch of a spotted salamander just revealed under a decaying log, the sensory power of the school of old catfish in my farm pond.

Blame old Henry Thoreau, if you wish, or Rachel Carson. When Aldo Leopold wrote *A Sand County Almanac,* I had to buy a ticket to northern Wisconsin right away. There were others, of course, and other seasons of discovery. They led to the Serengeti Plains of Kenya, the jungles of tiny Belize, the endless outer bank islands of North America. The Rockies and the Smokies eased my itching feet. There were sandhill cranes to bugle along the Platte River, flocks of whiter-than-snow geese gathering in Saskatchewan for their fall migration, and the twirping cry of bald eagles around Kachemak Bay in southwestern Alaska.

I have attempted to record my observations faithfully. They are my love letters, for my emotions still are stirred by such small events as a visit to my backyard by a flock of hungry wild turkeys, and the slow but deliberate arrival at my pond edge of the ancient old snapping turtle that feasted last summer on seven offspring of the resident Canada goose pair. Even now, in the late autumn of my years, my appetite remains unsated. Thankfully, the diet is nonfattening.

Don't say I didn't warn you.

Ora E. Anderson

Spring

Wind Borne

It's a tempered wind, this mid-March wind.
I trace its wanderings through the pines
And across the pond by
Its feathery burden of snow
(Light as the thought of your lips).
The geese call and inscribe their
Reflections in the water
Only to watch the tracery erase itself
In the wind's path.
Finches follow the snow currents
From tree to feeder to tree.
It's a mid-March day, all right.
Finches and snowflakes and waves,
And memories
Ride the wind to the palm of my hand.
Only the memories remain.

Restless March

MARCH IS A RESTLESS MONTH. UNCERTAIN OF ITS tomorrows, it moves under the gray cloud cover that already is far to the east, moving across the Appalachian ridges to shade the beaches of Maryland and Virginia.

March is a fickle month. Reluctant to admit that April is somewhere down my wandering little lane, it loosens wind gusts that ruffle the feathers of the various robins and redwings that came home yesterday.

Little clusters of crocus hover in the lee of my old workshop. A lone dandelion is no more than a drop of gold paint spilled on the ragged lawn. A cardinal moves up to the top margin of a nearby hawthorn and vocally lets the world know that it has lived fairly well through the trials of another winter without being tempted to head for the Gulf shores.

Parenthetically, I should point out that I deserve a bit of credit, too. I buy the feed; I built the trays where the corn and sunflower seeds are spread in major portions throughout the familiar neighborhood.

March is a month of promises made but not notarized nor marked by the official seal of the state of Ohio. Its certainty lies in its changefulness. Its dawns and dusks offer free samples of behavior that might be reminiscent of May or November or of other springs long past.

My pocket garden, still covered with the withered weeds and waste of last summer, must remain untouched for another week—another month, perhaps. Until April agrees that it's time to find my old rusted spade-fork and turn the soil for another season.

But my patience wears thin. Cloudy skies or clear, these days are measurably longer. The buds on my willow are putting on weight. I could hear the spring song of the rufous-sided towhee this morning even before I went outside to scan the sky and measure the accuracy of my thermometer.

March, above all, is an impatient month. It seems unsettled, unsure of its road map to tomorrow. It may have forgotten that I am ready for April now. Tomorrow, if things go well, it may remember to open that gray, gray cloud bank over east and let the sun bless me.

And then again, it may not, for this is March—restless, fickle, full of idle promises that hold no guarantees. It seems to match my own changing moods, my own uncertainties of hours and days, of senses and seasons.

As I ponder this moment, this changing of the guard between the dusting of snow that came last evening and the reluctant sun that is promised for tomorrow, I find it all acceptable—even welcome.

Spring Washes Its Face

THE WORLD HAS A SCRUBBED-CLEAN LOOK THIS
morning. The slanting rays of sunlight burnish a high gloss
on the dark green leaves of rhododendron bushes along
the far pond shore. Slender trunks of white pine cast parallel shadows along the hillside, straight and sharp as though
drawn by an experienced architect. On the muddy water
of the pond the rays of light slash across the perpendicular reflections of the trees, as though the rising sun can't
make up its mind what abstract pattern it wants to draw.
Light and shadow, shadow and light.

There's a hint of frost on the deck rail. A little flock
of dark-eyed juncos picks incessantly at minute tidbits
scattered underneath the hanging feeder. I note that their
flesh-pink bills match the color of their feet. They look so
cold, so exposed, so barefooted. They need new shoes for
Easter Sunday.

To this date in March, rain has tested the endurance of
everything. One more inch and there goes the neighborhood. Already the weatherman reports total precipitation
more than four inches above normal for the year. The

soil is saturated. The showers of yesterday and last night are on their way downstream somewhere. They found no place to rest, no porous earth, no thirsty leaf detritus to absorb them. Nature's sponges are full.

Just now the sun has topped the crown of trees along the east ridgeline. And now the temperature rises sharply. The light is brilliant. For a few minutes it reflects diamonds among the frost particles, then hides them in the darkening melt of warmth.

This is a morning that should be recharging my old batteries, stirring my adrenaline, starting a footrace among my red corpuscles.

There are important things to do today—tasks that should not be subject to procrastination. I must search for the great horned owls' nest that is surely located in the woods on my neighbor's land. Their frequent daytime calling comes from right-over-there. They converse loudly and sharply with each other. Some sounds are like the barking of dogs. I hoo-hoot in reply. They respond promptly. Later today I'll look for their bulky nest cavity, for the whitewash of their droppings, for bone and hair pellets, for stray bits of feather and fur.

A few days ago I found the demolished remains of what appeared to be a broad-winged hawk. The large barred wing and tail feathers lay under the massive branches of two ancient white oaks that shade the northwest arm of the big pond. In a long lifetime this is my first observation of a hawk as prey. Quite probably it was the victim of these same great horned owls.

But there are other items on my agenda. This should be a good day to transplant some trees. There are, for instance, four two-year-old seedling Japanese mulberries growing strongly in the shrubbery bed. Already they stand at least three feet tall and are elbowing each other for space. They come from seeds that a friend gathered under a productive fencerow tree near Antrim Park in Worthington, Ohio. I now have several of their siblings scattered around the farm.

In years to come, catbirds and robins, mockingbirds and waxwings will welcome the fruit and seeds that the female trees are sure to produce. As a footnote, this is the variety of Asiatic mulberry favored by the silkworm. Brought to this country in the nineteenth century to support the dream of a silk industry, the "white" mulberry has proved to be a prolific invader, but not a nuisance.

Unfortunately, our native black or red variety, *Morus rubra,* has become rather rare throughout its Appalachian range, and appears to be somewhat endangered. Only one healthy specimen is found here on the farm, a five-year-old female that already is about twelve feet tall and competing for space and light with a larger scarlet oak. Unless I can find and bring in a male tree for cross-fertilization, there will be no fruit.

How well I remember its rich flavor, its dark purple-red elongated clusters. In those earlier years I seemed to have found it fairly frequently, although it was never a tree of groves, and, like the butternut, might never have been very plentiful. When Harriet and I bought the farm in 1956, a very large native mulberry tree stood in an old fencerow on the central ridge, a fence that had divided the hayfield from the brushy pasture. For two or three years the "berries" of late summer made this old tree memorable.

Back to the day's agenda. Much of this afternoon was spent in futile search for an owl nest or signs thereof. Accompanied by my friend David and another young naturalist whose name I can't recall, I checked at least one hundred trees before finding one with an obviously large nest far up in its crown. Although there were no droppings, pellets, or other signs around the base, still it looked likely. We debated. We considered. We speculated.

So, with no further ado, David proceeded to climb some forty feet up a nearby tree to a point where he could see across into the nest. It was vacant. It showed no sign of recent use. Dave came down disappointed and somewhat breathless. The young naturalist said not a word.

Searching for the owl's nest proved so diverting that I completely forgot a committee meeting I was supposed to attend at four o'clock in the McArthur Public Library to help finish plans for a wood carvers' show scheduled to be held in that fair community later this spring. No worry, however. All committees work better in my absence.

Time now for sorting the day's junk mail, scanning the *Messenger;* reading the Monday one-day-late *Monitor;* further perusal of *Into Africa,* a colorful account of research into the lives of lions, baboons, and chimpanzees in Tanzania by Craig Packer; and, finally, preparing a most satisfying and filling dinner of crabcakes, shredded fried potatoes, Big Chimney bread, and cold buttermilk. On the outside chance that some inner space might remain, I partook of a generous helping of ice cream and sweet, sweet strawberries.

Now my agenda is full.

What Bird Is That?

I AM AN OLD, OLD BIRD CARVER.

Now, that is not an important or historic announcement. The mere fact that more than three thousand wooden replicas of wrens and warblers, cardinals and catbirds, have come out of my dingy workshop during the past fifty years may have added little to the subject of ornithology or the ultimate size of my bank account.

But let me count the days—after sweeping this clutter of wood chips from my shop floor.

Being a bird watcher is nothing new, of course. That all began in my far-off teen years down in the worn old hills of eastern Kentucky, while watching the strange courting flight and listening to the equally strange calls of a yellow-breasted chat.

In retrospect, now that my birding travels no longer reach into the foothills of the Rockies, the dry, dry valley of the old Rio Grande, or along the record tide margins of the Bay of Fundy, it is not surprising that my carving knives and tiny sanding devices have kept my memories alive.

An old bird whittler must remember that we are blessed by at least forty varieties of sparrows in North America alone. From the tiny Le Conte's and Savannahs to the impressively large lark sparrows, their size must be recognized to a fraction of an inch when a carving pattern is cut on the band saw from a pliant section of native basswood.

I love sparrows, despite their often-irritating similarities and subtle differences in feather patterns. In those early years, when my carving knives and observations were both sharp and accurate, realism was the rule. If the Peterson field guide said that a white-crowned sparrow could reach a length of 7½ inches from bill to tail tip, that became the workbench law.

Although our eastern rubythroat was the common order for those who wanted a carved hummingbird, more than once on my own I tried to produce a replica of the tiny Calliope, the West Coast native that is less than three inches in length and sports a scarlet-striped throat. Good fortune down through the years gave me sightings, but no orders, for the black-chinned and rufous varieties. Quite a big family, the hummers.

Although waterfowl decoys lured me to numerous carving shows in Ocean City, New Jersey, the eastern tip of Long Island, and down New Orleans way, for some reason I never became a dedicated duck hunter. The three families of Canada geese that were hatched and reared around the ragged old ponds on my home farm this spring can attest to that fact.

However, upon my shelves sit row after row of wood ducks and mallards, blue-winged and cinnamon teal, a pair of wigeon, and a lovely canvasback! Long years have gone by since they last floated around an old hunting blind in an East Coast marsh.

But let's talk about the warblers, those little feathered jewels, numbering at least fifty varieties, which find their elusive way north each spring. From the comparatively big yellow-breasted chat to the minute common yellowthroat, they sometimes seem to move north with the sole purpose of frustrating the army of bird watchers that heads for the well-known migration routes.

What evolutionary impulses, I wonder, produced such varied beauties as the red-faced warbler, the black-throated blue, the cerulean, and the Blackburnian? The nest-building styles of the ovenbird and the waterthrush fascinate me. I envy the old, long-departed ornithologists who claimed the right to name them for themselves.

Remember Swainson, Wilson, Bachman, Brewster, Grace, Blackburn, Kirtland, and Townsend? Perhaps such names are as colorful and appropriate as worm-eating, yellow-rumped, and black-throated gray. I'm perfectly satisfied that I came along far too late to have first identified a turkey vulture. Can you imagine an Anderson vulture?

From the longer perspective, of course, the wonderful birds that I have never seen often bring tiny twinges of regret—but not for long.

For I treasure memories of watching a dipper walking into the swirls of a mountain stream in the Rockies. Once I sat for more than an hour on a dry Dakota plain, waiting for members of a colony of burrowing owls to poke their heads out of their holes to satisfy our mutual curiosity.

I can never forget watching the broad, threatening front of a great thunderstorm sweeping in from the west and driving before it thousands of sandhill cranes looking for sanctuary along the shallows of the Missouri River.

Now every old page of listings; every map of far-flung highways, rivers, and marshes; guides bearing the name of Golden or Peterson; and every treasured copy of *Bird Watcher's Digest* tucked away on my dusty shelves, restores bits and pieces of precious memories of ducks and dunlins, swifts and swallows, and the old tom turkeys that have returned to our ancient Appalachians to spread their great fantails and signal to the hens that it's spring, and time to think about a new family of poults.

Pardon me, please. It's time for me to go out and fill my seven bird feeders. The cardinals are hungry, as usual, and impatient as well.

Birding Memories, Past and Future

My memory is quite selective. I seem to have little choice over its wanderings, especially now that an accumulation of multiple years leads to a more sedentary lifestyle.

With some difficulty, and with a modicum of frequency, I stumble along old familiar paths here on the farm, conversing quietly with newly arrived redwings claiming their nesting and foraging territories along the greening oxbow marsh. Here their numbers are few, not at all surprising because it is spring, and exclusive territories are essential.

Still, while listening to their rolling liquid calls yesterday, I suddenly recalled another time when their numbers were multiplied uncountably. It was in a chill November, at least a quarter century past. I sat in a long-abandoned duck blind, sunken among rustling, browning cattails, in one of the remaining marshes that necklace the southwestern shore of Lake Erie. Off toward the east, well beyond the plumes of smoke and vapor from the power plants of Elyria and Cleveland, the sun had just begun to show its rim of gold.

Then out of the vast wetland, like ribbons blowing in the wind, came streamers of birds—redwings, grackles, brown-headed cowbirds, starlings—all obviously headed southeast from their overnight roosts in search of grain fields, where the farm harvest was complete but scattered corn could still be found and where the seedheads of late-season grasses and forbs were plentiful.

For a few moments I tried estimating their numbers. It was an idle gesture. For more than half an hour the streams of birds flowed south in a noisy flood. Then slowly it diminished. Only a few procrastinators brought up the rear.

A few days ago two old friends, both addicts of open spaces and birdsong, joined me for a few leisurely hours of aimless wandering along familiar trails. Two pairs of pre-nesting Canada geese took note of our passing along the edges of ponds and marshes. Six mallards moved away across the open water, then sprang into nervous flight down valley. As we rounded a reedy point, a pair of wood ducks exploded into flight, crying plaintively over this interruption of their brunch time.

Again, I remembered another time—another place. More than seventy years ago, when legs were young and all horizons were limitless, along a wandering willow-lined stream in the eastern Kentucky hills, I went looking for pools where bluegills and eight-inch creek chubs might be found. Tiny darters, masked by rainbow colors, swam erratically in the clear, unpolluted water.

Then it happened! A pair of woodies, the first I had ever encountered, sprang from a hidden pool ahead and rapidly disappeared around the next bend, trailed only by their fright cries.

That was at a time when wood ducks were truly scarce. Old-growth forests were long gone. Ancient trees along creeks and rivers, offering nesting cavities for these most beautiful of North American waterfowl, were almost non-existent. Many years would pass before closed hunting seasons, artificial nesting boxes, and the regeneration of riverine habitat would restore their populations so old birders like me would not have to depend on memory alone to see them.

But where do the barn swallows now go to nest? The ancient, sagging barn that snuggled down in a protected hollow when we bought this old farm more than forty long years ago is gone. It collapsed into a pile of broken oak beams and yellow poplar siding a good quarter century ago. Its dusty hay had protected the homes of dozens of these graceful acrobats of the air each late spring. Down at ground level, at least one pair of phoebes always claimed the top of sagging sill log for a secluded nest. But, no more. Their descendants have moved on.

Little greenback herons always have been around in my wanderings along hill country streams and remote vernal ponds, where wood frogs and salamanders gathered and minnows were heron delicacies.

But not the great blues. Decades ago, in this land "up north," and quite probably south of Mason-Dixon as well, these stately herons were a scarce commodity. Not exactly endangered or threatened, perhaps, but not seen with the wonderful frequency of today. Even in winter, when ice entraps our minor river, there is always a hunch-backed

great blue standing forlornly along some open pool, waiting with the patience of Job for a school of minnows to swim conveniently by.

I miss the meadowlarks that once were a certainty in the sloping hayfields where redtop and timothy and a scattering of red clover shared space with field daisies, butterfly weed, and goldenrod. Now I must wander farther to find the wide-open spaces where larks can find perfect nesting cover and perfect fenceposts from which to call.

But, that's the way birding is. The riches of yesterday are replaced by new treasures today—and tomorrow.

It's easy to remember my first tiny saw-whet owl, which refused to budge from its perch deep in the arms of an old arborvitae in an extensive cemetery in Columbus, Ohio. More than a dozen watchers gathered around to see it blink sleepily at our intrusion.

Many years ago I sat for an hour and tried to sketch a half-hidden least bittern along a marshy cove of the Aransas Pass in northeast Texas. Another twenty years would pass before another posed for me here at my own pocket marsh. The memories now merge, and I don't mind at all.

Growing old has a bittersweet quality. I'm sorry to have missed the north Atlantic seabird colonies, the haunting call of an ivory-billed woodpecker, and the thunder of wings of a million passenger pigeons.

But there are compensations. As I write, all is quiet at my feeders because a sharp-shinned hawk came by moments ago trying vainly for a feathered lunch. They will return, of course, these hordes of cardinals and chickadees, white-throated and song sparrows, titmice and jays. Robins inspect my lane sides and meager lawn. Bluebirds are inspecting the man-made housing. Already the old mother goose is brooding her current clutch of eggs on the old nest platform at the head of the pond.

Memories of past birding are wonderful. That's a fact. I have more than my share.

But there are a lot of tomorrows. I plan to remember the pair of dark little swamp sparrows that were diligently working the water surface weeds at the island pond yesterday. And the great horned owl, relentlessly chased down the floodplain valley by a flock of indignant crows. The old gal had made the mistake of leaving her nest in a high sycamore when I came into view. A few crows took notice and soon called in dozens of noisy reinforcements.

On the way back home I stopped at the little cluster of old sugar maples and tried once more to identify the exact cavity where a pair of barred owls carried on last summer. No luck this time either—no prey feathers, no regurgitated pellets of fur and bones. But they are there. I *know* they are. So I'll be back for another visit, and another memory.

Early Mist

Suddenly, like thoughts in half sleep,
Wood ducks appeared in the morning mist.
Three—no four—drew curving lines
On muted water-canvas,
Tree-framed in lime green and sun gold.

Where had my thoughts spent the dark hours?

Devious Ducks

ORDINARILY ATHENS COUNTY, HERE IN THE HEART of southeastern Ohio, can hardly lay claim to being a prime stopover for migrating waterfowl. Those colorful flocks of bluebills and canvasbacks, as well as blue and snow geese, seldom vary far from their historic routes from the southern Gulf states to the marshes and pothole lakes of Canada and the Dakotas.

But that's a general statement. Always, there are exceptions. Few pintails and mallards, blue-winged teal or wood ducks, follow absolutely rigid routes from here to there and back again. On the other hand, no one can deny that the Atlantic coastal states, the great Mississippi drainage, and the eastern and western slopes of the rugged Rockies easily form the most traditional flyways for our feathered friends who favor cattail marshes over hillside pastures.

Well, there are exceptions! On this day in mid-March, a flock of at least three hundred lesser scaup, en route to the Canadian prairies for summer family duties, settled in for a day or two of rest in a most unlikely spot right here among our rugged old Appalachians.

First, the specific area in question features rolling hills and gentle wooded hollows. It has been sculpted and barbered by a fine, progressive, and successful real estate developer intent on creating a community for folks who want to live close to nature and can afford to pay for the privilege. So, off a major highway, reasonably removed from a minor airport and a sleepy village, the terrain has been brushed and polished, and subdivision lands and lanes are well laid out.

Then an invitation must have been extended to all migrating waterfowl to drop in for a visit. Across the barbered, rolling terrain are ponds, big and small, ponds that have not one historic relation to the area being developed.

It is common, of course, for waterfowl to flock together in migration. But not in our hill country! I have seen thousands of snow geese grazing on the browning plains of Saskatchewan. Great flocks of sandhill cranes have blessed my timely visits to the wandering waters of the Platte River in Nebraska. The twenty-year buildup of Canada geese here in eastern Ohio is nothing short of astonishing. But migrating bluebills—lesser scaup, that is—now, there is an uncommon sight in our little Appalachian backyard!

Yet here they were, hundreds of shimmering scaup completely covering a two-acre pond in the very heart of a new subdivision in Athens County, Ohio—far from any famous flyway from the sunny southland.

Undisturbed, they allowed me to park by the side of the crowded little man-made lake and watch them preen, dive for possible underwater food, and occasionally engage in a few romantic antics that will grow stronger and more frequent as they near their northern nesting destinations.

I've admitted this before: I am a very fortunate old bird watcher. It was almost anticlimactic when, within the hour, I visited a smaller impoundment, a landscape feature in the same nearby village, to study the watery wanderings of a snow goose, a mute swan, and a passel of Canada geese.

No, I really do not expect to discover an ostrich or a penguin feeding in my backyard with the great flock of wild turkeys that come for their guaranteed handout every morning. What're the odds?

Wading in Beaver Ponds

ONE RECENT SPRING DAY THAT SPORTED A PATINA of wildflowers and sunshine filtered through new unfolding tree leaves, I spent several hours wading around in beaver ponds. That's right—beaver ponds. In knee-deep mud and water, I tested my aging sense of balance while examining the engineering skills of *Castor canadensis.*

Actually, I am interested only peripherally in beavers. In this instance I was exploring the attraction that their secluded, wooded ponds hold for various birds.

In other words, I waded in, through, and around four or five such impoundments in search of birds that find such habitat to their liking.

Bird watchers are apt to consider this perfectly normal. Well, normal or not, the wading was rewarding.

Along a southern Ohio road from Mineral to Lake Hope, through Zaleski-Waterloo State Forest, several beaver ponds are easily found. One was an exceptional engineering feat, and at the risk of falling on my face and dunking my camera and binoculars, I took several close-ups of the long curving dam and lodge.

Resplendent wood ducks were in residence in the crystal-clear backwaters. Cavity-nesting birds found ample homes in the snags of trees killed by the beavers. First are the woodpeckers, of course—downies, hairies, red-bellieds, and an occasional family of gaudy redheads.

These leave behind vacancies for bluebirds and chickadees, titmice and nuthatches. Prothonotary warblers, one of the loveliest of the clan, find the combination of water and nesting holes irresistible, as do the graceful flying tree swallows, with their iridescent blue-green backs and wings and snow-white breasts.

Turkey vultures and red-tailed hawks rode the thermals above the wooded ridges. Yellow-rumped warblers and redstarts moved among the willows. Late trills of spring peeper frogs echoed from the marshy edges.

Some old men play golf. I wade in beaver ponds. It takes all kinds.

Mid-April Morning

GOLDFINCHES CAME TO BREAKFAST TODAY DRESSED up in yellow calico and black jackets. Two chipping sparrows wore rusty red caps so bright I thought the sun was shining. Cardinals take turns with their solos between sunflower snacks.

They want it both ways and I'm willing. The old Canada gander is about to become a father once more. He and his patient spouse, due to bring off their seventh new brood about April 18, hold big family reunions each winter at Lake Snowden. Dinner is potluck. Find your own. Can they recognize, or even remember, all those offspring?

The marvelous wood ducks that raised themselves on my home pond last summer have been coming back every day for the past month to collect their corn-flavored assistance checks. They know exactly where the cashier's desk is located.

Hungry visitors this cold gray morning form a varied lot—five squirrels, a pair of rufous-sided towhees, two crows, a dozen cardinals, four song sparrows and the chippies mentioned earlier, finches on the gold standard and finches decked out in raspberry red. There are blue jays, naturally, and nuthatches, woodpeckers in white and black, and woodpeckers with bellies red.

There's action—and color—and song.

Time enough for my second cup of coffee. With cream, please.

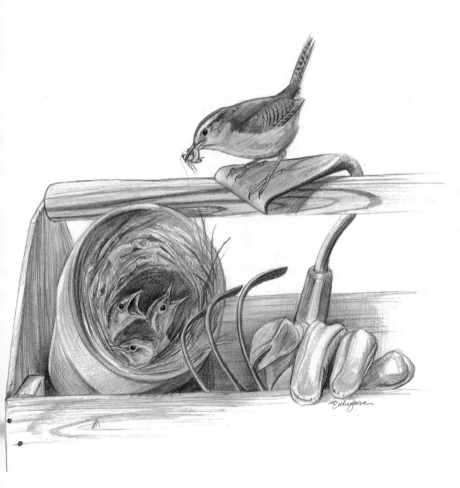

Old, Old April

So many springs have passed me now
With sweet sound of birdsong
And peeper chorus,
The drum roll of sudden showers,
And cloud fleets coursing
blue, blue skies.
My vintage wine comes
In old, old bottles, yet
Still sweet to the tongue,
With flowers of yesterday.

A Day in Early May

THIS DAY I MUST RECORD BEFORE THE SLATE OF my errant memory is wiped clean.

I sat on the low bluff above the horseshoe curve of marsh that, like a changeless fingerprint, marked clearly where an ancient creek once wandered. Reeds and rushes and the stalks of cotton grass poked up stiffly through the still waters. A few cattail clumps were exclamation points, and on one a red-winged blackbird clung.

Blackberry canes were still bare. Only the scattered mounds of multiflora rose gleamed green with new growth, promising their strange mixture of beauty and pain and, like humans, laying claim to their space solely by right of occupation.

Over in the tangled fencerow along the railroad, a mockingbird was using its entire extensive vocabulary to proclaim its territory. The continuous shrill of chorus frogs was strangely perfect in its disharmony with birdsong.

The morning wind was gentle. The dry grass and brittle stems of last year's goldenrod whispered around me, remembering the snows and ice of winter.

Three turkey vultures sat on the tie arms of power poles, their wings slightly open, waiting for the morning thermals to lift them into drifting spirals across the far ridge that rims the river valley.

The sound of a flicker hammering on a hollow snag came sharply form the nearby woodlot. The staccato rattle announces to the world that it's time—time to think of nest holes and mating and family responsibilities.

The hum of morning traffic rolled softly from the distant highway. Far off, up valley, the flat bleat of a diesel horn announced the approach of a train on its way from the Kanawha Valley of West Virginia, with its serpentine trail of cars burdened down with coal and chemicals.

As the sun climbed up out of a low bank of eastern clouds, tree swallows and their rough-winged cousins circled in like a troupe of ballet dancers, twisting and turning with acrobatic grace. Breakfast obviously was a morning batch of insects.

Listen! From way over there, beyond the old floodplain, beyond the row of giant sycamores, from the grove of pin oaks that border a shallow vernal pool, I heard the discordant call notes of a yellow-breasted chat, my first this spring, and memories came flooding in. This is the bird; this is the non-melody of sound that marked the beginning of my long, long years of watching and hearing and loving birds. This is one promissory note that I have tried, with mixed success, to repay.

And then, down across the old weedfield that anchors the eastern slope of the farm, came a marsh hawk—a female northern harrier. Its wing beats were slow and deliberate, almost mothlike. Cruising just above the crown of the tallest vegetation, it undulated with the slope of the land, lifting up and over the higher bushes and clumps of emerging trees.

Suddenly it dropped to the ground, hidden for an instant, then came up clutching a mouse. It flew to an old post in the line fence and proceeded to enjoy a late breakfast—or an early lunch. With wings spread in semiprotection, it displayed the brown marking on its back, the clearly barred tail, and pure white rump, exposed like a hanging shirttail. Through binoculars I could see its facial ring of lighter feathers, and the "eyebrow" line.

Admittedly, harriers are not exactly rarities in Ohio. I manage to locate a few each year, usually over the broad sweep of reclaimed strip mine lands in east central counties, or over the great wet meadows that mark where the ancient preglacial Teays River once ran.

But to me this was a special bird. This old hill farm has borne my name and tolerated my wandering footprints for more than five decades, yet on this spring day, in this late autumn of my years, this is the very first visit to these wrinkled acres by *Circus cyaneus,* the northern harrier— at least as seen by me. It will be a while before the memory fades.

The Virtuoso Brown Thrasher

Listening for long moments to the vocal performance of a brown thrasher is an experience to cause any bird watcher to ask for an encore. It bears repeating, on and on and on. To hear the clear, flowing notes and phrases of this remarkable long-tailed songster is quite an experience: I could almost call it an epiphany.

From perches high in tangled thickets all up and down the hills and valleys of all our eastern states, this cousin of the vainglorious mockingbird and the more nasal-toned catbird fills the courting days of May, and on into June, with non-stop harmonies. The notes of its melodies follow each other like falling water—clear, liquid, continuous.

No, this is not necessarily a daily performance. This soloist follows no set schedule or playlist that I can discern. But every spring, when avian romance is rampant, I always hope for a happy accident, an unexpected perfect bit of timing when, on a quiet walk along the tangled edges of a thicket of blackberry canes or hawthorns joined in well-planned barricades, I suddenly hear this outpouring of thrasher music. I stop in mid-stride. Momentarily I hold my breath. Somewhere, hidden, there is a vocalist singing of love and romance and the joys of nesting time. In my mind's eye, I can visualize its slender ten-inch form, fox-red from head to long, flowing tail. Its yellow eyes detract not one whit from the subtle gray of its cheeks and the regular rows of black spots from throat to rump. Each wing, I know, sports two handsome white wing bars.

Now, all this purple prose means no disrespect whatsoever to all the other members of the thrasher family that bring musical scores galore to our southwestern states from Texas up through Arizona, New Mexico, and into southern California. The smaller gray sage thrasher is even more widespread in its range in the more arid portions of California and Nevada.

Some bird guides go so far as to proclaim this smaller cousin an even sweeter singer than my hometown brown thrasher. I can't buy that, although, being an old easterner, I haven't had the privilege of crawling into a tangle of cactus to hear a solo by a gray thrasher.

My life list does, fortunately, include the curve-billed thrasher (seen in the Big Bend country of Texas), but I must admit that not once have I positively, unquestionably, indubitably seen the spectacular California thrasher, or those other southwesterners—the Bendire's, Le Conte's, and the red-rumped crissal thrasher. I scan the pictures of these remarkable birds in my dog-eared field guides, and wonder if they, too, are world-class vocalists.

At my age and state of decrepitude, I'll probably never know for sure. So, that being the case, my choice is still our handsome, and still champion, the one and only brown thrasher.

Three times in my long life I have been privileged to enjoy a very different kind of performance by this bird—once as a teenager, again several years ago, and more recently this late spring.

In each instance I was attempting to find a thrasher nest. The movements of the birds had given me some indication that it was nearby. I moved as slowly and stealthily as my innate clumsiness would allow.

Suddenly I heard the song, and just as suddenly I discovered the nest, deep in a tangled thicket, and fewer than twelve feet away. The notes were mere whispers, clear but muted, as if coming from perhaps acres away.

The bird was sitting on the nest! Her bill was slightly open. Her throat feathers pulsed to each song phrase. This was no song designed to attract a mate—this was a melody of quiet joy, of contentment.

For long moments I listened, mesmerized. In each of these three experiences, separated by years of joyful birding here and yonder, I was able to finally slip away, leaving the beautiful singer undisturbed.

That's it, friends. The brown thrasher can sing for me any old time, anywhere, and I'll pay the price of admission.

Early June Troubles

My calendar says it's early june. the sun, this bespangled morning, obviously agrees. The leaves of a spreading sweet bay magnolia, reaching up from near the corner of my back deck, reflects the light from down east and shares it with a hundred of its creamy white blossoms. A tiny wisp of steam floats up from my morning cup of coffee.

Three mourning doves scavenge for thistle seeds under the hanging tube feeder, which is shared at this moment by a pair of polished goldfinches.

The deck railing, spread with its usual breakfast menu of sunflower seeds and cracked corn, has attracted all of its regular customers—cardinals, chickadees, titmice, squirrels, and chipmunks.

As titular head of the Anderson Benevolent and Protective Welfare Agency, I am responsible for all of the above. No question about it. My monthly bill for bird and animal feed, including that for eleven hundred and eighty-three hungry bluegills in the nearby pond, leave me nothing to invest in the perils of Wall Street.

But there are flaws in this colorful fabric of nature. My troubles are many, even though they should come as no surprise. Let me count the ways.

Three families of Canada geese (six watchful parents and eight big, fat youngsters) live right here in my yard and claim full title to the pond that reflects the light and shadows of the towering pines on its south shores.

Now, friends, these are big, healthy geese. They have unlimited appetites, and *very* healthy digestive systems. They also have friends, many friends, in the form of ten to twenty other geese that, although full grown, were too young to have families of their own this year. They, of course, claim their share of my property and my largesse.

So, it is hardly surprising that my deck must be hosed off every day. I walk with watchful care and trepidation across my well-fertilized lawn. You should know that my extensive lawn areas couldn't be used by great seed companies or manufacturers of fancy mowing machines as classic examples of perfection. Weeds are plentiful among the more desirable grasses. Haphazard clumps and rows of jonquils, always expanding, must be left undisturbed until midsummer in order for me to admire their thousands of golden blooms next April and early May. Yet at this moment in June every plant looks tired and worn, obviously ready to call it a day.

The family of groundhogs that wintered under my deck has now established a summer home in a far corner of my yard. The hole is a hazard to old fogies like me who wander onto remote areas of the farm from time to time. The old resident rodent shows no concern for my welfare.

A few days ago I inadvertently left the gate to my little vegetable garden open. Within hours the greening rows of lettuce and peas showed obvious signs that either the groundhogs or a neighboring cottontail rabbit had been enjoying a fresh salad. I'm a slow learner.

With amazing regularity, this spring has brought a wonderful balance of rain and sunshine, windy storms and gentle breezes. Sounds great, doesn't it? Green is my world's popular color. The girth and height of maple and oak, hickory and ash, dogwood and hemlock all along the ridges and benches of these old hills are testing their limits of growth.

But not all has been calm and peaceful. Thunderstorms have come rumbling in since early April with unusual regularity. Wind gusts have tested the age of old fencerow trees whose growth rings easily pass the century mark. Several of them gave up the struggle and came crashing down. Now they lie tangled and broken. My chainsaw and splitter will turn them some fine day into stacks of cordwood for my fires of December.

The old creek that wanders through the lower reaches of the farm has been restless, too. Flooded by the generosity of these April and May storms, the currents have tested their boundaries more than once, flooding out of their worn channels and washing out over the low bordering fields where corn and timothy once grew. Last year's crop of great annual weeds now lies flattened, tops pointing uniformly in the direction of the current's flow.

Dead tree limbs litter the wooded ridges and lower slopes. The trees self-prune as they grow in girth and age. It's a natural process, but there seems no end to the task of clearing the debris from my meandering trails and woodland margins.

In times gone by, when one could draw on seemingly endless sources of energy, the planting of trees was simply a matter of choice—how many to tuck into the moist soils of March and April; what varieties to favor—walnut or oak, poplar or hemlock, maple or one more version of willow.

But trees wait for no man. As they grow in vigor and girth, as their crowns reach up and up for their share of the energy of sunlight, they push their own limits of space. Year by year they illustrate with embarrassing clarity the fact that, twenty years ago or forty years ago, I planted them too close together in the great open spaces of those old scrubby pasture fields.

Now they are in serious need of thinning. Their trunks need space for fattening into muscular logs. Their crowns need room to spread their individual canopies of green over the understory of trillium and bloodroot, rhododendron and ebony fern.

Here I find my mirror image. My years, too, are as many as the oaks that may remember where the old fences once ran—between gardens and hayfield, between cornrows and pasture lands.

I walk slowly. The sun is warm on my sloping shoulders. The breeze from down valley brings the call of a wood thrush.

So, I offer up my litany of troubles this day in early June—the hungry geese that shed their molting feathers around my ragged lawn, the scars of groundhog dens, the never-ending hunger of wild turkeys, white-tailed deer, and the scores of cardinals, jays, and chickadees that come to feed around my little kingdom.

But I exaggerate—it's obvious that these are not troubles. The weathered swing seat on my pond edge eases my aching back. I swing my old binoculars up to follow the circling of three turkey vultures against the proscenium arch of blue sky.

My fly rod stands in the corner nearby. I'm tempted to cast a bit along the pond edge, where dozens of big fat bluegills are gathered. Not a bad idea for a tasty lunch, friends.

Come on over and share in the travail of a happy old man.

Quicksilver

I wrestle with the days,
So brief they are,
So strong in their resistance
To my reaching hands,
They slip through my fingers
Like quicksilver,
Like the last light of
mid-May dusk,
stealing off into the woodland,
hiding in the arms of midnight.
Even their memories now elude me.
They skip away
With those who are young,
With those who can dance
To rhythms I no longer hear.
Still, new mornings come
And for brief moments
Lie warmly in my arms.
I touch their shining faces
With longing fingers.

Summer

Fairy Dust

The dust of fairies traces the path
Of moths that beat their fragile wings
Against the windows of my night.
They seek not me, but just the lamp
By which I write.

What draws you here? A dream,
Or just a momentary beam?
And will you leave no fairy dust
Across the windows of my life?

Birds Along the Hocking

WATER IS A MAGNET FOR BIRDS. REED-GROWN marshes, farm ponds, spring-fed brooks and meandering rivers all attract residents and migrants of the avian world.

Our old hill-country Hocking River is no exception. Great blue herons stalk its sandbars and cutbanks or stand motionless along the muddy margins in patient hunt for minnows and frogs. Green-backed herons, less spectacular in size and coloring, exhibit the same ability to remain silent and motionless in their foraging habits.

Kingfishers patrol the river bends, sounding their rattling alarm calls when disturbed. Barn and tree swallows hawk the water surface in fluid grace, harvesting mosquitoes and myriad other flying insects.

June is a great month for canoeing our old river to see the frequent families of wood ducks that make their homes along its more placid currents. This most lovely of waterfowl has made a remarkable comeback from near extinction some fifty years ago.

Mallards, too, find nesting sites as well as winter havens of open water, particularly along the "big ditch" from White's Mill through Athens.

Even an occasional migrating osprey enjoys fishing the Hocking, especially in fall, when the water is like crystal and the fish can be seen easily in the shallow pools.

It's a right fine old river. Just ask the birds.

The Chat

I SUPPOSE IT SHOULD NOT SURPRISE ANYONE, looking at my hands and other clues, to learn that I have been carving various and sundry birds out of pliable wood for more than forty years.

In my own retrospective view, this was perhaps inevitable. Shall I start from the beginning?

Okay. I became a bird watcher at about age eleven. It happened one July day, in the old wrinkled hills of Boyd County in eastern Kentucky. I was picking ripe, luscious blackberries in the far pasture when a strange bird, about yay big, bright yellow on the breast, green-gray over the back and head, suddenly flew up out of the berry canes near me, and with a strange fluttering style, flew perhaps thirty yards or so before landing in similar tangled thicket. Throughout its flight it uttered a continuous song that was neither melodious nor poetic.

Here was something completely new to me.

As I continued to pick berries, this same bird repeated its strange flight pattern and song several times.

As soon as I came home, I began a search for the identity of this new feathered friend. I had no bird books of any kind. No one in my family was able to help. So, I went down the country road, stopping at several neighbors' homes, asking for help. Finally I located one of the small palm-sized books that were then the nearest thing that might be called a true field guide.

And there was the bird of my blackberry patch—a yellow-breasted chat.

Even the somewhat amateurish illustration made identification easy. White eye rings. Bright yellow throat and breast, no wing bars, and a rather long tail. Its entire upper body was an interesting dark greenish-brown. And, surprisingly, it was listed as a member of the warbler family—in fact, the largest member of that colorful clan.

As subsequent years went by, I slowly came to the realization that this bird, this yellow-breasted chat of those old Boyd County briar thickets, was one of my most important discoveries ever, for it sparked a lifetime of birding that has led me across the far prairies of America, deep into the western mountain valleys, and along sandy beaches and rocky shores from Maine around to Oregon.

Although it seldom wanders as far north as the Canadian border, the chat summers through all the states east of the Rockies and winters as far south as Panama. Only during its nesting period, usually late May or well into June, can it be seen with some degree of regularity—but especially when romance brings on that strange courting flight and staccato solo by the yellow-throated male.

Most of our tiny and colorful warblers, although lovely in every way, are hardly noted for their singing abilities.

In spring migration only the most dedicated ornithologists can surely identify species by their lisping, often slurred, notes. Sometimes the sounds are like the calls of insects in midsummer. But they are welcome sounds—even those of the yellow-breasted chat.

For I know, too well, that their lisping melodies of spring will be stilled in September, when they head southward dressed in muted colors that only hint of their courting feathers of April and May.

Gentle Hours

LIFE IS GOOD! PERHAPS I SHOULD CAPITALIZE THAT statement, underscore it, put it in boldface type—or at least in italics. As an old man in my nineties, I'm in a position to know. Good fortune dogs my footsteps. Morning sun, filtering down through the trees that hover over my trails, lays a gentle hand on my shoulder.

Birdsong still caresses my somewhat diminished hearing—the liquid notes of the wood thrush, the invitation to tea from the rufous-sided towhee, the soft tremolo of bluebirds.

This old southeastern Ohio hill farm, bald and wrinkled after a century of subsistence farming, rewards my forty-plus years of benign intervention with goldenrod and golden finches, morels and meadowlarks, and the sighing wind in the crown of towering pines and poplars.

Are there problems? Of course! The Biblical Job had crises that I can relate to.

Every new tree I plant must be protected, immediately, with a covering of wire. Otherwise they will be eaten off or battered by my neighbors, the resident white-tailed deer.

Woodchucks invade my garden. Raccoons seem to know at once when at night I fail to close up the tiny greenhouse where I store bird and fish food.

A pair of beavers insists on damming the spillway from my home pond—every night, in fact. And every morning I must breach it. Muskrats undermine my lawn, having found or made openings in the underwater retaining wall. The Canada goose family, now in its seventh generation, over-fertilizes the grass where I must walk.

My battles with multiflora rose, poison ivy, panic grass, and Japanese honeysuckle never seem to end. Beetles devour the leaves of my grapevines and the blooms of the great clumps of marsh hibiscus. Horntail spiders float their midsummer webs across all my trails—at eye-level, no less. Mosquitoes and deer flies, midges and chiggers conspire against me. A new type of caterpillar is rapidly denuding my catalpa trees. Mice are invading my bonsai collection. Chipmunks claim generous portions of sunflower seed that is intended for cardinals and chickadees.

But not to worry. I know where the wild rose is still blooming. The dusty pink crowns of joe-pye weed mock the midsummer heat. A fidgety pair of Carolina wrens has just fledged their second family of the year from a nest in a hanging basket of hoya vine outside my sunroom window.

There'll be a full moon tonight. It will be coming up in the east just as the sun slips behind the western ridge. I must be there for the curtain call, while my admission ticket is still valid.

Evensong

A wood thrush sang on my forest stage,
Then two—
Then three!
Liquid as quicksilver,
The notes rolled down the valley,
Settled onto the mirror pond surface,
Melding liquid to liquid
Without one ripple.
Dusk closed the curtain so very slowly.

Looking Back

CAN A CHILDHOOD MEMORY REALLY BE RECAPTURED? Who can attest to the accuracy or the excitement of a remembered high-school romance? When young were my years, did every April rain force a sea of trillium into instant bloom up every wooded hollow? Was every song of thrush delivered in perfect pitch and harmony?

Such idle questions really do not call for uncontested answers. For instance, what has accuracy to do with the numbers of nighthawks in migration flight across a distant Kentucky ridge in 1927? I stood open-mouthed in wonderment that September day.

Never again have I seen such a flight of these spectacular birds. The score of worn field guides on my back-room shelves make no mention of such a spectacle. Uncounted bird watchers annually record the thousands of hawks and eagles that follow the ancient Appalachian Mountains or the shorelines of the eastern Atlantic states, with no mention of mass flights of this cousin of the whip-poor-will. Was this an illusion on my part?

One day in an early June I sat at the edge of a beaver pond tucked away in my beloved southern Ohio hills. Dragonflies flew their erratic patterns back and forth along the reedy margins. I swatted idly at an occasional hungry mosquito. The flow of water talked its way over and through the wandering dam of sticks and mud.

Then, from upstream, came a pair of hooded mergansers, with nine downy young—a flotilla that was as strange in this area of Ohio as it was beautiful. In past years, only in border states and on the backwoods lakes of Canada had I been privileged to watch such parades of summer.

I remember when English (or house) sparrows were considered a major nuisance around busy farmyards and grain elevators, where spilled wheat and corn, oats and barley, provided an endless banquet. Their bulky nests filled every opening under the overhanging eaves. They are still here, of course, many generations removed from their European ancestors that came, as did we, to seek new horizons. Their numbers now are easily counted.

Paradoxically, the same evolutionary path was followed, within memory, by the lovely house finch, another newcomer from Europe. Imported last century to both of our American coasts, it found the New World a welcoming place. With song and beauty, it claimed new homes in new neighborhoods with amazing speed. Even in our central states, its population exploded in the last years of the last century.

Then, tragically, a contagious eye infection reduced their numbers dramatically. I can only trust that somewhere out there, from San Francisco to Brooklyn, from New Brunswick to New Orleans, they may find an immunity that will bring their cheerful song back to my neighborhood.

But I worry a bit about such old Appalachian natives as ruffed grouse and bobwhite. Their numbers have fallen substantially as the forests have returned to our eastern states. Here are bird families that relished the farming practices of the early 1900s—smaller grain fields, ragged fencerows, weedy pastures, the wild grape and blackberry tangles that preceded the amazing regrowth of our hill country forests.

Apparently the state wildlife departments haven't noticed this changing population. The open seasons and bag limits remain at the same overly generous level as that of a quarter century ago.

But I notice. My little farm is a microcosm reflecting this habitat change. At least ten years have passed since the sprightly call of a bobwhite or the spring booming of a grouse has echoed across my ridges or from my old weed fields and tangled fencerows.

Obviously, I want it all. Three years have passed since I last heard the sharp, repetitive call of a whip-poor-will.

Where is the pair of great horned owls that built their massive nest in the forks of an old sycamore down along the creek that wanders through my lowland? For nine years they raised their annual pair of big-eyed, downy youngsters here. I never charged them a cent of rent, but they're gone now—hooting in some other hollow, I presume. Oh, well, there are still compensations.

At least four families of wild geese will find welcome homes around my ponds each summer, this I know. Already those past puberty are noisily pairing off and courting shamelessly each morning, when the flock of thirty or forty comes sailing in on set wings to accept my hand-outs of corn.

The local contingent of wild turkeys arrives even earlier, dropping down from their night roosting trees at the first light of dawn. Four old gobblers lead the way. More than thirty sleek young ones of last summer come loping in like anxious colts, fully expecting me to have the grain already spread across my ragged backyard.

It's an old, old story, of course. Whether we humans are guilty of wiping out a hundred million passenger pigeons or the last ivory-billed woodpecker, or of saving the California condor from the edge of extinction, is probably an idle debate.

But, see, my problem is obvious. I want free-ranging buffalo, an occasional moose coming down to my pond to feed on water lilies, and the sight of a bobcat slipping along one of my old trails. And, of course, there's room here for a pair of trumpeter swans.

Is that too much to expect, for heaven's sake?

Well, maybe. On subjects like this I can be pretty unreasonable at times.

Rubythroat

In soft sunlight
It lay in the palm of my hand,
Its rich red throat feathers
Rising, falling, shimmering, pulsing
To the beat of its hurting heart.

Seconds ago, in weedy fields,
It found the sweetest flowers.
The brightest colors caught its eye.
My feeder dripped false nectar
Too close—too close to my window
Where it fell.
Now light as down
It lies in my hand.
Heavy are my thoughts.
Does my love, too, have a ruby throat?

The Geese Fly Now

July 3—THE GEESE CAN FLY NOW. THIS MORNING, standing on the deck of the cabin, I saw them take off and fly the length of the big pond. Fully feathered and full grown at four months, they had been faithfully practicing for the last three weeks, and now they were free to explore a new world, the air, the sky.

July 5—At seven o'clock the sun already is warm on my shoulder, the promise of one more ninety-degree day. The breakfast dishes, such as they are, have been cleared away. The book on my table is *The Good Rain* by Timothy Egan, who writes eloquently of the northwest corner of the nation.

Through the screen door I hear the first clamor of the Canada goose family. Down they come, over the eastern line of trees, seven curving black lines silhouetted against the sky. Their big yellow feet, like airfoils, drop down to take the first impact on the water of my home pond where they were hatched and, for the most part, raised.

These geese are no strangers to me. This is the fifth, and most successful, year that this same pair has nested on my pond. Three times they used the tiny weed-covered island as a nest site; twice they have used the elevated box platform that I built for that purpose in the shallow upper end of the miniature hill country lake.

They are not very good parents, this pair of Canadas. Oh, they're faithful enough at nest building and suffering through the long weeks of incubating the eggs, but when their downy goslings arrive on an April morning, all common goose sense seems to go out the window.

Within twenty-four hours of hatching, the little flock, usually numbering from five to seven, is led away from the safe confines of the pond into the surrounding weed-choked old fields nearby. Is the motive fear of exposure to hawks and owls, or wrinkled old snapping turtles? Are they seeking more open waters where the sightline is less limited than on this small, forest-enclosed body of sparkling water? I don't know.

The result, however, is predictable. Each year one or more of the struggling little goslings is lost in the weeds and underbrush. In past years, never more than two have been raised each spring. This year, however, five out of an original seven have survived to adulthood, handsome in their gray plumage, with white chin straps, breasts, and rumps. I never tire of watching them go from here to there like a miniature flotilla of in-line ships, leaving a growing wake on the mirror surface of the pond.

They have become tame, accustomed to come for the corn and bread and floating fish food that I put out twice daily. They vary their own diet, however, grazing (and fertilizing) the grass of my lawn, stripping weed and grass seeds from the summer-ripening plants, and dipping in the shallows for whatever a lucky goose might find there.

In early June the adult pair molted their flight feathers and for a while were as immobilized as their offspring. Now, however, in early July, they are once again strong flyers, ready to rejoin other small flocks on the larger reaches of Dow Lake, Lake Snowden, or along the Hocking River.

Their comings and goings are stirring, yet the calm routine of their life around the ponds here on the farm lends a sense of serenity to the passing days.

Come autumn there will be a growing restlessness to their wanderings. Their flights will be to farther fields and waters. Their flocking instincts will be stronger, more pervasive.

I know, however, that their bond is now strong to this little valley, to this tiny pool of water that reflects the surrounding pines and ash trees, the oaks and maples, the vagrant clouds.

So, as the weather cools in the waning months, when the maple leaves are gold and scarlet, when the oaks are great mounds of maroon, the geese will return.

Quite likely they will bring with them a passel of relatives and friends, gathered up from other farm ponds in the surrounding hills, from golf course lakes and highway borrow pits, from strip mine waters and wooded streams.

They know a good thing when they find it. They have learned that around here there will be no booming of shotguns at dawn, but there will be generous handouts in the form of corn and stale bread and a share of the pellets that are thrown out to the local fish.

And when winter locks most of the other scattered waters in thickening sheets of ice, this, their home pond, will have its usual pool of open water, kept that way by a faithful man-made air compressor that will bubble up its supply of warmer current from the depths of the pond.

These geese have it made.

Waning July

Evening arrived early in my little valley today. July seems reluctant to leave the summer stage, but I am well aware that only a handful of its days remain.

There is complete stillness reflected in the green-shaded mirror of the pond surface. Across the way, thick clumps of rhododendron hide the bases of tall white pines. Seedling ash and soft maples hover quietly around the trunks that stand tall and silent against the background hillside.

As darkness grows almost imperceptibly, I listen for late birdsong, but none sounds from the higher ridges or down valley, where older hard maples and sycamores mark the line fences and trace the deeply cut vein of the creek.

The clarity of the calm, unruffled pond water is painted more deeply green by the reflection of tree seedlings and woodland undergrowth that relish their share of light around the open water.

Earlier this day I walked through the weedfield that slopes sharply upward from the western side of my little house, making note of the ranks of field daisies, orange coneflowers, and coreopsis.

Here and there, small, determined clusters of red clover and alsike seem to bloom for the sole purpose of reminding me that they are hardy remnants of the old farm pasture that ruled these slopes so many seasons ago.

Only one member of my wild goose flock has kept me company this day. Hampered by a lightly injured wing, he was reluctant to fly off two days ago with his raucous and numerous family and friends who have failed to show up for their lunch or dinner.

Again I listen for birdsong, but even the cardinals that lead the way to my feeders are quiet. August is due next week. Nesting time is over for my friends, the chickadees and titmice. The wood thrush and robin are still. Even the jays are unseemly quiet.

Although the sun ventured through a break in the cloud bank at midday, it found no welcome. All afternoon and now into early dusk, the sky is solid gray. If there is a weather front in the coming night hours, it seems reluctant to disturb the evening's calm and silence.

Last night I listened to the steady fall of rain that brought an end to too many days of dryness. In the darkness I heard neither the bluster of wind nor the roll of thunder.

It was easy to sleep.

If you suspect that I am partial to the rains of summer, I offer no denial. There seems to be a special quality to a July storm that sweeps in from the southwest and drums its way through these tangled woodlands, bending the loaded seedheads of tall grasses and the yet-to-bloom goldenrod and ironweed in the open fields.

I will remember this day, this hour, when September paints my hillside with the golden shades of tulip poplar, when the rugged maples are scarlet and the oak leaves are browning.

Small families of scaup and teal may swing down for brief rests on my inviting ponds and marshlands on their way from the Dakota and Canada pothole country to the remote waterways of the Gulf states. They will be welcome. Of course, I am somewhat of a dreamer—an old optimist.

If the stillness of this early evening promises the liquid song of a wood thrush, the sharp call of a bobwhite, or the wavering whistle of a screech-owl, I never expect a guaranteed performance in July. The time for avian romance is pretty well over for this year.

But there will be other quiet days in October, when only the rustle of golden leaves falling from my old maples and tulip poplars will whisper to me. The ridgelines will begin to show through the thinning foliage. There'll be little clusters of late-blooming asters along the lane, as I drive down to see what my utterly charming mail lady may have left for me that day.

An autumn love note, perhaps?

The Sound of Longing

THERE IS A QUIETNESS ABOUT THIS MORNING—
a hush that can almost be heard. The soft sprinkle of rain-
drops, more mist than droplets, seems to emphasize the silence. No breeze is moving. The crowns of the pines are
still. Usually they signal the slightest movement of air, the
arrival or departure of any vagrant breeze.

The sky is still overcast, not with the great boiling
stormclouds that moved through last night, leaving every
leaf one shade greener, but with a solidity the color of old
pewter that has sat on some dusty shelf for too many
years.

It is midsummer but something is missing. I have yet to
hear the wavering, rasping buzz of the first cicada. Here
is an insect that defines, for me, the days of July and
August—the shimmering heat waves over a distant highway, the rolling echoes of thunder, and the orange crowns
of butterfly weed along an old fencerow.

Am I premature in my expectation? Will the strident call
come tomorrow or next week, or is this one more sound

of summer that may be fading into memory? I hope not. Too many such losses already are listed by my senses, and in my census records.

Three years have passed since I lasted listened at nightfall to the piercing call of a whip-poor-will. Not a single honeybee has come this year to the wild roses and honeysuckle, or the varied blooms in the old weedfields. I heard no grouse booming in the spring woods—this year or last. Yet I listened on more than one April morning.

There are some surprising and exciting listings to offset the growing scarcities. An old hen turkey now wanders the woodland with her growing flock of poults, leaving torn patches of old leaves in their search for insects and grubs, weed seeds, and softened acorns.

The familiar pair of Canada geese already has left the home pond with their four full-grown youngsters and joined the bigger flocks that are building up on the larger lakes in the area. They'll be back, come ice-up time.

Wood thrushes may be scarce elsewhere, but not here in my old hollows. At dawn and in the evening's growing shadows, they still sound their liquid flute notes, although nesting time must surely be over by now. It's the season of the young—the time of year for restocking our supply of chipmunks and cardinals, of chickadees and titmice. Juvenile doves, resplendent in their spotted and white-edged feathers, come to the feeders and wonder where to start. The young cardinals have an unfinished look—their bills still dark, their topknots in disarray. Newly fledged red-bellied woodpeckers are as slender as *Vogue* models, as uncertain as high-school freshmen.

The blackbirds, their epaulettes now pale yellow with little trace of springtime scarlet, are joining the expanding flocks of grackles that come to clean out my supply of cracked corn and sunflower seed in record time each and every day.

Here in mid-July the young crows, now completely mature, no longer forlornly call all day long for food from overworked (and probably impatient) parents.

All the young wood ducks and mallards around the local ponds and streams have learned to fly—and they obviously love it.

Bloom buds and clusters are forming on the tall joe-pye weed, the marsh hibiscus, the purple ironweed, and the spikes of goldenrod. An old Virginia creeper vine that completely covers the trunk of a pond-edge tree across the way is already turning scarlet. The leaves of buckeye trees are looking worn and weary and soon will be leading the late summer color parade.

But I want to hear the dog-day buzz of the cicada— the tremulous rise and fall of its mating call. After all, this is midsummer, and I'm running short on patience. Fireflies are dandy, but they don't have the wolf whistle of a cicada in search of a mate.

Lost—By Choice

ONE NEEDS TO BE LOST NOW AND THEN—
momentarily disoriented, a traveler on an unfamiliar trail.
Clouds may hide the sun, giving no hint of the direction
north—or the direction home. What lies around the next
bend, across the next ridge, down the slope of the next
valley?

The stream along this wandering stretch of gravel may
not have a name. It gives no hint of its destination, only
an impression of reluctance to hurry—a need to slow its
pulse while watering the roots of willows and river birch,
of sycamore and ironwood.

Call it a hobby, an idiosyncrasy, if you wish, but I
search for just such scenes. I follow little wandering township roads through the hills of spring and autumn,
through the generosity of summer and the spare bareness
of winter. They start from nowhere, these little-used lines
on my maps of Athens and Meigs, Vinton and Jackson
counties—and they go nowhere.

Yet all along the way, on ridges where county lines go
unmarked, where old abandoned railroad beds are slowly

collapsing from age and disuse, I seem to find exactly the place I need to be. Lost-ness is its own reward.

There is such a road. I travel it all seasons. Early on it led me astray, willingly, though I had no idea where it might enjoin with another lane or highway.

In fact, there are scores of such enticing byways all through our beloved hill country. They beckon you into Waterloo and Zaleski state forests, through ancient sandstone-rimmed valleys in Jackson and Vinton counties, or across the broad plain where the great preglacial Teays River once ran on its way from Virginia to a mysterious destination beyond Dayton, Ohio.

Northern harriers and short-eared owls now skim over that once-mighty riverbed, harvesting mice and voles. Red-tailed hawks and kestrels share the bounty.

Ferns grow lush in the still woodlands, where an unhurried little township road wanders its way from Mineral to Lake Hope, hesitating here and there as if intrigued by beaver ponds and small colonies of red-headed woodpeckers.

I know it well, this road. There's a vantage point from which to watch great blue herons fish for frogs and carp in an old swamp created jointly by beavers and the fill of the now-abandoned railroad. I walk through the tunnel and listen for echoes of the lonesome wail of steam engines that once served Mineral and New Marshfield and now-vanished Luhrig.

Mountain willows grow rank in the swales. Wood ducks raise their broods in beaver ponds where painted turtles sun on half-submerged logs.

Colonies of red-stem lady fern compete with the glorious fronds of cinnamon and interrupted fern. Little clusters of Indian pipe spring up after summer rains to mark where trillium and ramps ruled in April and May.

If I am lucky I can revisit the coves where showy orchids reach just above the leaf mold, and partridgeberry hides tiny white bells under dark leathery leaves.

Some of these roads show me where pawpaw and hazelnuts are October-ripe, or where raspberries and wild strawberries tempt my tastebuds in July.

What's on your schedule next Saturday morning? How about visiting Buffalo Beats, the tiny prairie remnant near Buchtel, to see if the seedheads of bluestem and rattlesnake master are ripe? The pale bottles of green gentian may be in bloom.

Or perhaps we can walk the bike path (slowly, of course) and watch for the towering blooms of cup plant and wild sunflower along the old right-of-way, or study the snowy tangles of wild buckwheat vines commandeering their territories.

In another few weeks the wave of warblers will come winging out of the north, revisiting the thickets and tree crowns along my favorite township roads, where I watched their passage last April and May.

Gotta go now!

Night Shadows

Night shadows resist the first light,
Crouching behind the hemlocks,
Hiding in the fern ravine,
Fighting a rearguard retreat
Up the west hollow.

The last to go crouch here beside me,
Holding me hostage 'til daylight
Storms my bedroom.

The dawn can't come too soon.

The Passing of August

ONE MORE DAY REMAINS OF THIS AUGUST. AT 6:15, dawn is still wiping sleep from her eyes. Fog has painted everything pale gray—the far shore of the pond dimly seen, the dark trunks of pines are like out-of-focus prints by an amateur photographer.

There is no stir of air, not a single rustle of leaf or wand of goldenrod. Reflections in the pond mirror are mere suggestions. They lack clarity, reality, definition. A bluegill breaks the surface and it is almost an illusion.

I step out onto the deck of my little house and the muted sound of the opening door disturbs a great blue heron at the far end of the dark valley. With the soft beat of its great wings it moves off through the fog, a ghost bird against a ghostly backdrop of soft pines. A wood duck whines and springs out of the shallows, disappearing instantly in the mist.

It is wake-up time. I fill the feeders that were emptied by last evening. I spread cracked corn in generous helpings across the back lawn. At the vibrations of my footsteps, hundreds of bluegills gather from all directions, moving with hungry impatience along the pond's edge. The dim shadowy forms of great catfish move in the underwater background, almost unseen, moving in their own version of fog.

Water drops have gathered on the ragged grass of my lawn, harvested from the fog in more generous quantity than the normal dew point could have gleaned. The earth is soft from recent rains. I walk out quietly to spread the morning bounty of seeds and grains. I cannot sense a single bit of sound from my slow, deliberate footsteps, yet it is clear immediately that vibrations from each step must transmit themselves through the ground, even the wooden retaining wall, and into the still pond water, for dozens, even hundreds, of bluegills swim from all directions toward the stretch of shoreline where I will throw their feed. Those near the surface, barely seen in the dim light and green water, make approaching curves of ripples.

I throw out handfuls of floating pellets, scattering them widely. The feeding frenzy begins. The smaller fish are delicate in their eating manners, but not so the twenty or thirty old channel catfish. Like automated vacuum cleaners, they cruise just under the surface, mouths agape, scooping in the floating food. They seemingly do not use eyesight to help locate the bounty. Just by cruising back and forth, they engulf generous quantities from the scattered feast. Often they collide in their random maneuvers, breaking away with vigorous thrashing of their broad tails. For long minutes until the food is gone, these irregular collisions and splashings are the only sounds that break the stillness of the early morning.

Strangely, the bass and crappies do not take part in this feeding ritual, although they share this little bit of sheltered water lapping softly at the roots of pines and maples, rhododendrons and marsh hibiscus. Obviously they prefer their more natural dietary selections of tiny minnows, unlucky grasshoppers, and other forms of lively protein that share or fall into their watery domain.

I do not hurry this morning ritual. I fill the feeders with sunflower and thistle seed. I scatter generous quantities of grain in the patches where grass is sparse across the backyard. Small excavations and tiny holes tell me that field mice and chipmunks also are opportunistic diners, competing with the impressive flock of wild turkeys that will come by soon, their white heads and bronze backs moving erratically as they eat rapidly of the scattered corn.

Now, off to the east, the sun has begun its invasion of the fog bank. There is only a soft glow at first. The light freshens. Although the gray mist is still heavy, the minute water droplets obviously are catching colors of pink and yellow, miniature rainbows in suspension.

As the valley becomes less opaque, and shrouded trees become individuals instead of melded shapes, the birds begin to arrive. Cardinals first—bold scarlet males, muted females and their offspring of the passing summer, appearing suddenly out of the foggy nowhere. Titmice and chickadees flit in like electric sparks, each selecting a seed and darting to some preselected nearby perch to hold it in tiny feet, pry it open with tiny bills, swallow the sweet, sweet kernel, and return within seconds for seconds.

And here they come, my extended family. Blue jays, redwings, house finches, grackles, and soft mourning doves that look like bits of fog themselves. Goldfinches fly in to hang suspended from perches on the thistle feeder, selecting the minute black seeds that, for all they know, may have come all the way from India.

Song sparrows search the ground beneath the feeders, knowing that the sometimes ill-mannered and aggressive flocks in the high trays will spill bits of their provender over the edges.

Two little greenback herons can be dimly seen working the far waterline, their concentration and slow stride matching the silence of the moment. Suddenly the sun finds a weak spot in the defensive wall of fog. The lights come up across the eastern stage. As if on cue, a great flock of noisy grackles, glistening adult males and motley brown females and young of the summer, come clattering in like a dark thunderstorm—a hundred at least—perhaps twice as many. Who can estimate the noisy, jostling mass of aggressive hungry invaders? Only a few of the more stubborn doves hold their positions at the dinner table.

Within minutes the supply of seed and grain is gone, the trays bare. I step quietly outside to refill the feeders, but my black visitors take off en masse, like the sound of a sudden storm front. I am not trusted, obviously. Oh, well. In a very few moments my natives will return. They know the old man. He is quite useful and seems to know where seeds supplies are not only inexhaustible, but free. Why worry?

September Lament

A LL MORNING I AM TEASED BY TENTATIVE, ALMOST imagined, rolls of thunder, off to the west or over the low hills north. Now and then a quick slash of rain sweeps in, diminishing to a drizzle that ends as gently as it comes.

The wind, too, is unable to make up its mind, swirling from nothingness to gentle breeze to robust gusts that bring down more browning leaves of ash and walnut than drops of rain. Already many of the green ash trees that years ago invaded the old weedfield uphill from my house have lost most of their leaf cover, thanks to a bone-dry August and a less-than-ideal growing site.

I watch the weather maps with more frustration than despair, more wishful thinking than anticipation.

Hurricanes that blustered their way across the southern Atlantic, threatening the Gulf beaches and the overpopulated outer banks of the Carolinas, turned into pussycats with wet feet. They never made it to the Tennessee border, much less the dry bluegrass of Kentucky and the parched Ohio Valley, though they left a drenched and scrubbed-clean Gulf Coast.

The puny little marsh that the roaring bulldozers and backhoes created for me along the ancient, seasonally wet oxbow is pleading for rain to re-submerge its cracking mudflats.

Clumps of reeds and rushes that last spring stood knee-deep in freshwater shallows now have a hard time remembering the lush wetness of June.

Only the herons, little greenback and great blue, like what they see—a smorgasbord of frogs and minnows forced to congregate in the diminishing pools near the dikes and dam.

The old trees that stand where fences once ran, beaten by a thousand storms and scarred by bolts of lightning, are showing the stress of dryness. There are no acorns for the fox squirrels. Pawpaw trees will not hang low with heavy fruit this year.

I walk the trails to the far ridges and the rustle of dry, new-fallen leaves follows me like a raspy echo.

A red-tailed hawk atop one of the distant power poles screams shrilly. Maybe, just maybe, he is letting me know that this is his territory, that I am the interloper. His call, for whatever reason, matches the dry wind that moves through the dry grasses along the dry ridgetop.

Birdsong? I ask myself—is this more than the usual late-summer lull, the quietness that simply marks a season's change, a completion of family responsibilities, a prelude to migration?

Only a few hummingbirds still come calling at the sugar-water feeders on my deck, and they are forced to compete with swarms of yellow jackets for a place at the table. Within short weeks from this mid-September date, they may well be visiting the walled gardens of old New

Orleans or the backyards of Rockport, Texas, and the Rio Grande Valley.

The little creek that bisects the floodplain just to the east shows only remnants of the flow that filled it to the brim last April. Dry leaves float on the currentless surface like fairy boats with faulty compasses.

The tracks of those natives that come down to the water's edge to drink have baked hard and sharp in the drying mud—the knife-cuts of deer, the handprints of raccoons, the enlarged hind foot marks of muskrats, ringed by shards of sweet flag and the half-eaten roots of cattail.

The dry margins of the ponds and marshes no longer make a record of more light-footed visitors like killdeer and spotted sandpipers, song sparrows and marsh wrens.

Because I am not too smart, or because I'm driven by a shrinking time span, I have continued to plant specimen trees this summer: Kentucky coffee trees, silver bells, willow oaks, a ginkgo biloba. Now, under the rainless skies of August and September, I must carry water to keep them alive—gallons and gallons of water, dipped from the pond and carried from here to way over there. No wonder my back hurts and my aging shoulders are stooped. Or should I spell that "stupid"?

The weather maps offer no threats and few lukewarm promises of change for the (wetter) better. Perhaps I should walk my trails again and look for discarded feathers, turkey and vulture, owl and crow, with which to stage a rain dance up on the ridge, where the skeleton of a teepee still stands. My former neighbor erected those lodgepoles back when she went by the name of Kathy Yellowbraids. Perhaps she remembers the proper chant to bring on the thunder-filled clouds.

Whatever—I am tired of the dryness of late-summer dog days. I shrivel and wrinkle with more than just old age. I want my cup to runneth over, and not with pennies from heaven. I want to hear the pounding of a storm on the roof of my house, the swoosh of columns of rain racing across the pond surface, the sound of rushing water down every slope, every ravine. I want to see the inflow of freshness pouring into the ponds and marshes, swelling their desiccated bellies until they cannot hold another drop, and the spillways can drain the welcome surplus off into Factory and Margaret creeks and on into the Hocking and Ohio rivers and all points south.

That's not so much to ask, is it?

Thirteen Jays!

Thirteen blue jays;
Thirteen bolts of blue,
Slashes with black and white,
Came this summer morning,
Unannounced.

Only casually invited,
Muscling their ways to trays
Of seeds grown sweet
In July suns.

Bold, brash, ill-mannered,
They cleared their plates
And left without
Washing the dishes.

Fall

Letters Home

Prayer is like the whisper of dry leaves
On the forest floor, accepting the passerby,
The dance of sun shadow,
The birdsong in the towering oak.

Its answer is a sudden quickening of the heart,
A catch of breath
Exhaled like mist in the forest dawn.
The soaring hawk, riding a thermal,
Carries my plea skyward.
At my feet
The wind hurries the dry leaves homeward
Like letters borne by angels.

Lonesomeness

LONESOMENESS COMES IN LITTLE PACKAGES. Thoughts develop like a nagging toothache. There's no flavor to the coffee. It tastes like leftover leftovers. There's the wrong filler in the sandwich. It's like reading a good book that has a contrived ending, a creative lapse. Or, the plot is good, but there's a weak character wandering around in it.

This moment is very early morning. An old moon is a half-lit Chinese lantern in the still-dark western sky. The leaves on the ash tree outside my window shower silver coins that never reach the ground.

Quite probably this will be a good day—but not yet. Not at this very moment. It's time to feel the ancient ache in my back, the heavy numbing weight of my legs, the persistent wrinkles and lumps that have grown overnight in this swaybacked mattress. My mouth is dry from the long night of fitful breathing. There is no one here to touch softly, no tangled hair to stroke, no soft warm curve to explore.

Oh, well. In each day some thoughts must follow a few obscure dead-end trails. Sunup will surely come. It always has. And I know exactly where it will splash its first touch of gold leaf on the top branches of an old fencerow oak down the eastern ridgeline. When it does I'll cradle a cup of coffee in my hands, sit on the steps at the end of the dock, and watch the wisps of mist rising from the pond, wisps that are pleasant ghosts in the slanting rays of the new sun.

I'll contemplate, that's all—just contemplate.

Perhaps today will bring another surprise like yesterday, when three least sandpipers came in to explore the edge of my wetland mudflats—tiny, delicate, miniature, exciting shorebirds already on their way south for the winter.

And the blackberries are ripe down by the oxbow. I never have dark thoughts berry-picking. There are always diversions. Memories invade the process of selecting the ripest berries. It's a bit late in the season, but I will not be unduly surprised to find the nest of a field sparrow, filled with three or four wide-eyed youngsters ready to graduate from their avian grade school.

Perhaps, by pure accident, I may rediscover the old terrapin on whose carapace I scratched my initials more than forty years ago. Like me, he is pretty territorialized, for I have located him twice before in this same ragged old field during the last quarter of the last century.

If I am persistent, which is somewhat doubtful, there may be enough blackberry harvest to consider making a few glasses of delicious dark jelly. That's not really much of a chore. Recipes are tucked away in the little file box in my kitchen, reminding me how much water and sugar to add to the pot and how to judge when the cooking is completed. I'll drain the sweet juices overnight through a cheesecloth bag. Then next morning, if all goes well, I'll boil it gently in my old iron pot that has shared my storage shelves for more than fifty years. Now and then, I'll test the consistency of the thickening syrup by dipping a cold spoon into it. When it nears the jelly stage, the hot syrup will drip from the spoon reluctantly and slowly form a cover of pure sweet ambrosia.

Perhaps I'll have enough to fill four or five glasses, newly washed in boiling water, of course. There'll be hot melted paraffin to seal the tops before setting them on the edge of my kitchen counter where they will cool and slowly gel into treasures for December breakfasts.

Am I dreaming? Well, of course. Old men are apt to idle away many late-summer days relishing memories of berry-picking excursions into old ragged briar patches.

A ruffed grouse may explode from the woodland edge, leaving me in openmouthed wonderment.

Perhaps I'll find a great multibranched golden claveria mushroom—the edible kind, of course, or even better, a colony of delicious chanterelles.

Simply wandering along old familiar paths on this day fills my memory's pockets with the golden hearts of field daisies, the late song of an indigo bunting, the graceful cloud circles of a pair of soaring turkey vultures.

It's quite clear, friends, that my wealth is unlimited, even though it is scattered all over these old hills and along wandering creek beds. Often the search for it is my reward.

Giving Thanks

It comes as no surprise that the shadows of dusk move into my little valley a bit earlier every day. After all, it *is* September. The good Lord never promised that the dawn hours of late May would continue to bless me until it was time for a heavy frost—when November claims its place on my well-marked calendar.

Already the buckeye trees around these old ridges are beginning to shed their gold and browning leaves, for invariably they lead the autumn color guard.

A family flock of blue-winged teal settled down on one of my welcoming ponds this morning. These lovely little waterfowl are well known for heading south to the marshes and bays of Mississippi and Louisiana far earlier than mallards or canvasbacks or other birds of the Canadian pothole country.

Soon my old overgrown fencerows and woodland edges will come alive with busy smaller visitors, en route as usual to the Gulf states, the dry mountains of Mexico, and the jungles and plains of South America. Their colors are not as bright as they were in spring. Their songs and calls are less frequent and more muted, because their family time has come to its climax for the year.

I refer, of course, to the ever-active movements of tanagers and warblers, flycatchers and swallows, all now feathered in the muted colors of autumn in sharp contrast to the brilliance of their April and May plumage. These are hours to remember—days in which to give thanks, to count blessings, for those most certainly are numerous.

Remember how late summer often brings visitors, sometimes unexpected, but welcome nonetheless. Good fortune may have encouraged our own wanderings; vacations along the sunlit beaches of the Atlantic, visits with that great collection of old cousins down in Kentucky, an exciting flight across the plains and mountains of America to once more look down on the amazing land and seascape of San Francisco.

It's hardly necessary to remind ourselves that one of our favorites of the holidays that brighten our lives and our calendars is Thanksgiving—with a capital T. It is just offshore a bit, just down the road and around the next week on the calendar.

What a wonderful time to remember the good years that have come our way, the precious children and grandchildren that add sparkle and zest to our days, even sometimes beyond our diminishing tolerance and patience.

So—as I contemplate my own waning tomorrows, as I enumerate the seemingly endless blessings that have come my way, I have no desire to list my numerous little problems—the ache in my back, the halt in my step. There are more important things to do.

One of my granddaughters just called to say she is coming down to the old farm to spend the weekend with me.

In my mail today was a photograph of my very youngest great-granddaughter, wearing a wide-open smile—at six months of age, mind you.

So go our days—our years—filled to the very brim with blessings that only our Heavenly Father seems capable of bringing.

As one more Thanksgiving rolls around on the cooling winds of another November, it will be pretty easy to agree that it is well-named, this special occasion—with emphasis on the "giving."

Eighty-fourth Birthday

I T'S NOT HARD TO BE OBJECTIVE ON ONE'S eighty-fourth birthday. Whatever will be will be. All those yesterdays have added up into an accumulation of pleasant yesteryears, half forgotten and tumbled together like old shoes in my bedroom closet. Like memories, some of them are too good, too comfortable, or too useful to discard, and there's nothing to be gained but a bit of space if the others are tossed away.

Not that it is easy, or even possible, to completely discard a memory. Merely noting moments of the past brings them bubbling up in the mind like a well-done stew, rich and tasty with the spices of childhood, the mystery of puberty, the joys of romance and love, of family and career, of iris and ferns, of birds and mountains and outer bank islands.

This day has a special quality to it. I have read and reread this small stack of cards from those whom I love deeply. I wonder sometimes what I have done, or said, or been to have earned these greetings and good wishes.

The morning is washing its dusty face with a steady downpouring of rain. After weeks of dryness, the ground is greedily satisfying its thirst. Wind gusts sweep haphazardly across the pond surface and the old weedfields and into the woods, shaking down showers of leaves. Many trees—especially the walnuts and ash—already are bare.

This will not be an autumn remembered for its colors.

But there are benefits. Because of the weather, my calendar is clear. Two appointments have been cancelled, one by a student of sculpture interested in creating something (who knows what) somewhere on the farm; the other by a Kenyan friend, who had hoped for another day of working in the woodlot, trimming and thinning, clearing tangles of wild grape and weed trees.

So I write—and dream—and remember.

Tomorrow will be another good day—more rain, perhaps measured in inches, is promised. The newly dredged wetland over in the southeast corner of the farm will begin to fill. Slowly the water level will rise, up the slopes of the island forms, out into the surrounding grassland, eventually to flow among the rushes and reeds of an old oxbow, where the creek used to run.

The new apartment house for purple martins is in place, as are the bluebird houses and the nesting box for wood ducks. I must stick around to see another spring—to witness the transition of the seasonal marsh to one of year-round shallow water that mirrors the season and plays host to spring peepers and leopard frogs, to redwinged blackbirds and the sweep of swallows on the wing.

I plan to watch for the first bloom of skunk cabbage and the golden mounds of marsh marigold in the seep below the foot of the dam. Their reappearance is more certain than my own.

It is a good day—this 30,660th of my life. And I am grateful.

The Lingerer

October says it well.
I lengthen stride to overstep a leaf,
Already turned to lace,
That paints a daub of umber on the path.

Beyond the garden line the latest storm
Has blown a gray and deadened elm to earth,
Its shattered limbs exploring holes
Where flickers homed in spring.

The goldenrods nod hoary heads today,
And crows hold noisy caucus in the woods.
A lone wood duck comes in to feed at dusk.
(It must have missed September's gulf-bound flight)

The air is cold. Three frosts
Have marched across the distant browning ridge
To mark the fragile fern and all its kin.

I know my own October well, and yet
I feel the sun of April in my heart.

October Omens

THIS BRIGHT MORNING HELD FROST IN ITS HANDS, placing it carefully on the deck railing, on the northwest roofline, and the low spots in the lawn. The thermometer registered thirty-six degrees.

By 8:30 there were no silver traces left. The accumulated warmth of the earth, stored from the day-after-day sunshine of late summer, wiped the puny advance of winter into oblivion. Temporarily.

Everything out there is getting ready for the long cold, the harsh, hard edges of winter. Cypress needles are a-browning, falling like moth wings down through the twigs and branches, catching in clusters to form hummingbird nests that will never be used. Slowly they paint the earth around the fluting trunks with soft raw sienna.

Clumps of zebra grass on the dam are waving their ripening seed plumes like a cluster of drum majors. Most of the ash trees and buckeyes have already dropped their leaves into hidden pockets of the old weedfield and are standing immodestly naked.

The creek runs low. Isolated pools harbor schools of chub minnows that dart for cover when my shadow walks by. Leaves and seedheads are gathering in spangled drifts against the open edges of sandbars and among the tangled exposed roots of trees that cling precariously to the top of the bank.

I watched for long moments as a family of bluebirds and several cedar waxwings industriously gathered the ripe seeds of Virginia creeper vine along an old fencerow.

Already the woods floor is carpeted with the early fall of maple, ash, and buckeye leaves. Hickories are rust brown. Oaks are hinting at the maroon of November.

There is some token resistance. The two violets I picked this morning look mournfully insignificant in the smallest vase I could find, yet their color is a good match for my front door. I found a sprig of yarrow in fresh bloom along one of the lower trails. While planting a clump of hardy pink aster on one of the wetland islands, I found myself standing in a mass of peppermint. The aroma lifted me off the ground. Airborne, I looked down at the ripening seedheads of vervain and smartweed, sneezeweed and coreopsis, and the hanging clusters of elderberry. It was difficult to come back to earth.

The last blooms of goldenrod are the color of tarnished brass. Even the late asters appear ready to give up their rearguard action and sign their seasonal surrender papers.

Any day now the white-tailed does and their fawns of the year will be hustled from cover to cover by amorous bucks that have been in hiding all summer. Their ability to remain out of sight is uncanny. The fawns have lost their spots and now wear soft brown coats overlaid with silver, as do all the adults.

This is the late fall of my own years. Some of the trails that lead ridgeward are more rugged than I remember on those early walks, when breathing was sweet and easy and my stride was long and strong.

Still, the sun is warm on my shoulders. The blue jay at my feeder is just as arrogant as the ones that came to call when I was ten, or forty, years younger. The ripple of song of the Carolina wren is no less sweet because I may not hear it as clearly now as I did yesterday.

I think I shall postpone January. In the meantime, I'll go measure the girth of a pine tree in the far woodlot and estimate how fat it will be when my great-grandson wraps a tape measure around it in 2050.

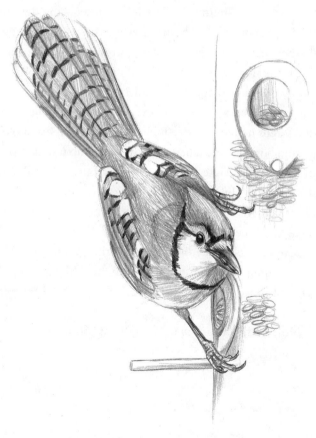

The Daytime Trip of the Nighthawks

I SAT ON AN OPEN RIDGE ABOVE THE BROAD VALLEY where the old, untamed Ohio River accepts the flow of the Big Sandy, which, in turn, serves as a convenient border between Kentucky and West Virginia. Across the valley to the northeast lay the placid hills of southern Ohio.

I was young then. Every bird in the old pastures and fencerows around me was an exciting discovery. Bluebirds and wrens nested in the leaning posts that supported old, rusting barbed-wire fences—even as they do today. More than once in the late spring days I had found, at eye level, the little grass-lined nests of tiny chirping sparrows on the lower branches of scattered old pine trees growing around the open slopes.

Screech-owls made their homes in the convenient cavities of aging beechnut trees along the winding little road where I drove our cows home for milking each summer day.

Now and then, as I wandered the old pastures, a flushing ruffed grouse or a covey of bobwhites demanded my immediate attention. In early springs, when avian romances were in vogue, rufous-sided towhees urged their mates to *drink your tea* in the tangled blackberry thickets.

My only bird guide was a little pocket-sized book produced far back in the early 1900s, plus an extensive collection of tiny picture cards found in every box of Arm & Hammer baking soda. My mother and several kindly neighbors saved them for me.

There were highlights, of course—multiple discoveries in those early birding adventures.

Migrating flocks of mallards, pintails, and blue-winged teal often dropped in for rests on the strange little town reservoirs that had been excavated along one of the ridgetops.

Every veteran bird watcher knows this story—there's a familiar pattern to it. Every new bird is a discovery worth noting, an adventure to be stored away among aging memories. Yet sooner or later, there comes a sighting so amazingly unexpected that it remains sharp and clear despite the passing of years. This is mine—unbelievably mine.

It was early autumn. Although the skies were clear, a smoky haze dimmed the far-off ridges above the old river valley. The year was 1927, a year seemingly created just for me, for I was nearing my sixteenth birthday. As I stood on that old hilltop, gazing off into the blue, I was suddenly aware that the sky was filled with a host of birds completely strange to me.

Unlike the great flock of grackles that gathered from time to time to roost in the wooded valley of the creek near our home, here was an obvious migration. A seemingly endless stream of brown, slender-winged birds, their white throats and barred breasts in full view as they followed the ridge southward just overhead.

For almost an hour I stood and watched as they passed. They were uncountable. The flight pattern of this feathered flock certainly was erratic, except in mass. Their obvious destination was southward.

My little pocket bird guide, studied at home that evening, gave me no guarantee of identities, but there were hints. White throats, white bars on the dark primaries, and their backs and breasts were a pattern of dark and light brown.

Even when I narrowed my search down to the page where the artist-author offered pictures of whip-poor-wills, nightjars, common poor-wills, and nighthawks, I was uncertain. Slowly, however, in my untrained but excited memory, I narrowed the field of possibilities.

The long, angled wings were sharply pointed and bore broad white bars across the black primaries. They extended well beyond the tail, which also was marked by a single obvious white bar. The illustrators allowed me to eliminate the chuck-wills-widow, the common poor-will, the whip-poor-will, and the buff-colored nightjar because of their rounded tails. The book said the common pauraque never came east of the Mississippi River. The lesser nighthawk stays far down in our southwestern states and Mexico.

I was coming closer—closer. This endless, erratic flock, this once-in-a-lifetime-scene—at least for me—had to be our common nighthawk.

I am now an old bird watcher. My excursions, perhaps like yours, have led me far afield in search of one more new discovery—one more new bird for my life list. But some firsts remain far more vivid in memory than others over the years. Those were nighthawks I watched that long-ago day on that old Kentucky ridgetop—an endless flight of common, but surely uncommon, nighthawks.

An October Walk

I<small>T'S MID-OCTOBER, AND THE TRAIL THIS MORNING</small> is carpeted with the discards of summer. I walk on whispering colors: scarlet and raw sienna, maroon and umber, and a hint of yellow-green.

The air is a benediction and the sky a proscenium arch of blue. Even my old bones ache less than usual.

On such a day, with such a pocketful of blessings, I can afford to luxuriate in the moment. Migrating warblers shopping for lunch in the fence tangles along the path take precedence over thoughts of firewood to be split and stacked by the wall of my shop. The old heating stove can wait its turn. Just now there are more important things to divert my attention.

Off to the north somewhere a flock of crows has found a sleepy old great horned owl and is shouting obscenities at it—defying it to come on out of that grapevine tangle and fight in the light of day. They sound excited at this moment, but the fun won't last; they'll soon drift off somewhere over the next hill and the next far valley, as crows always seem to do.

I follow the leaf-littered path down along the old weed-field. Ranks of goldenrod now wave tarnished banners. The dry needle pods of swamp milkweed hang in graceful clusters.

Little flocks of goldfinches, dressed already in their more somber fall attire, do their dipsy-doodle flight from one clump of exploding thistle heads to another, all seeming to agree that the next one must be better than the one at which they have been feeding.

As I walk along the dikes and trails around the wetlands, I note that song sparrows follow similar illogic. As I approach wherever they may be feeding or resting in total obscurity, they suddenly decide that a change is absolutely necessary. They dash out in their own erratic flight style and twenty yards away dive into hiding again.

Is one place actually better than another? All these secret spots look the same to me—dense thickets of vervain, milkweed, poke bushes hanging full of red-purple berries, clumps of button bushes, young sycamores, and reeds and rushes.

What's the hurry? I'm armed only with binoculars and a dog-eared bird guide. I silently ask the same question of a great blue heron that takes off in surprise from the edge of a marshy peninsula and flaps laboriously to some other less disturbed spot down the valley.

The resident red-tailed hawk screams from his perch high atop a dead snag on the ridge, advising me that I should get out of his territory. Quite plainly he is saying, "Go on home!"

Only the mockingbirds (and there are several) seem unruffled by my passing. It's such a lovely fall day, and all their problems of procreation are over. The youngsters of

June have gone off to some mockingbird college, and now it's time to sing again. I watch and listen as they move about in the hawthorn tangles, flashing their white outer tail feathers and wing bars, and trying on for size all the new tunes they picked up in summer. Mozart never had it so good!

Cautiously I approach the margin of open water still standing in the marsh. However, seven wood ducks see me before I see them. They spring into flight like gold and green rockets, complaining as usual in their high-pitched whines. Somewhere back in dim prehistory, their genes developed the knowledge that humans are not to be trusted.

Oh, well, they'll be back tomorrow and again the following day. In the meantime, I'll sit awhile here in the shoulder-warming sun and admire a small kettle of soaring turkey vultures, shifting their wings a bit from time to time to take advantage of every thermal updraft, every gust of wind from the west. Here we go again—just one more demonstration that the grass may be a little greener (or a deer carcass a little riper) on the other side of the next hill.

As I meander across the old floodplain meadow, following the aimless curves of the creek, I suddenly am aware of other wanderers. In fact they are in squadrons. Tiny aerial spiders, pinhead size, cling to the tips of twigs, on faded goldenrod spikes, and on the withered flowerheads of joe-pye weed. Each one spins a single strand of web that gains in buoyancy as it grows in length. Finally, I watch speechless as each minute arachnid chooses its own style of flight, drifting off to somewhere, anywhere, on its own silken parachute.

Only twice in my long lifetime have I seen the miracle of millions of such aerial spiders in mass flight, hemstitching the sun rays and blue skies together with almost invisible sparkling threads. Where are they bound? What destination are they seeking? I wander the trail homeward, stopping momentarily to watch a family of waxwings conducting a taste test in a wild cherry tree. A clump of startling blue-bottle gentians demands attention. I sample a cluster of fox grapes hanging temptingly low overhead.

Then back through the woods again, shuffling slowly through the newly fallen leaf litter, while an old doe and her teenage fawn of the summer, dressed in their cold weather brown-gray garb, watch me silently from only a few yards away. I think we have met before.

Funny, isn't it, how old things like October days, migrating warblers, and heron tracks in the mud seem always so new, so surprising, so ever-demanding an encore. I must go again tomorrow!

Reverie

The path through all the woodland still is fair
November winds still taste of vintage wine
The oak still grasps a leaf to give to spring
When winter's through. All these still pleasure me.

But in the midst of birdsong comes your voice
And my heart wonders at the melody.

At Last, the Rains

THE RAIN THIS MID-FALL MORNING WAS SOFT, A caress. It was still dark when the whisper of its wet fingers brushed the west window beside my bed. It was the kind of awakening that my aching bones and muscles long for but have been denied by the dryness, the almost unbroken aridity, of August and September and well through October.

The random patterns of leaves that had drifted down onto the pond surface this week slowly began to be submerged. Steadily the individual spots and splashes of gold and scarlet, umber and sienna, became waterlogged from the curtain of rain, finally sinking from sight as their wet weight overcame their buoyancy. I sat at the sunroom window for long, delicious minutes, cupping a steaming coffee, listening to the muted drumming on the roof, watching the breaking surface of the pond.

This rain has come belatedly, and its gentleness carries no hint of wind or cloudburst; nevertheless it set about its job of bringing down the summer leaf cover. In the growing daylight the woods across the valley are opening up, taking down the green curtains that covered them all summer. Now I can see the ridgeline, running from the lower trail at an easy angle up to where the oaks and maples, the cherry and ash trees are slowly but surely exerting their dominance over the pioneer dogwoods and aspens. Nothing in nature is static; there is dynamism even in a community of trees.

With the temperature lingering in the mid-forties and the cloud cover hanging low, even the birds share my reluctance to get moving, to face the day with plans and purposes. After I fill the feeders with sunflower seeds and scatter cracked corn on the ground, the usual cardinals and chickadees, the jays and doves appear to be in no hurry to brave the showers.

My beagle, kenneled up for the night, shows no impatience about a late breakfast. Not surprising, of course: A beagle is a notably laid-back creature, seeming to view humankind with tolerance and sly humor.

There is no noticeable diminution of sound, but I am suddenly aware that the rain has halted. The pond is no longer wrinkled and dimpled. The surface becomes a mirror, the glass dark, the light muted, yet the reflection of the ranks of trees and the slope of the ridge are clear and sharp, because the ground is covered with a blanket of color, of raw umber and rich scarlet, tucked up around the forest floor as if in anticipation of ice storms and zero nights to come.

Now that it appears to be ended for the day, this little rain, a meager ration after the long thirst, still must be noted as a small blessing, a promissory note, perhaps, for future payments on a dry ledger of deficits. For surely, with November at hand, there will be serious rain, determined rain, rain that will be reluctant to stop, slow to move on into the east with its clouds weighted down with water sucked from the Pacific and the Gulf of Mexico.

Wrinkles and cracks in these old fields will drink and swell shut. The forest floor will fill its leaf sponge with all the water it can hold, and then send the surplus downhill, always downhill, into every tiny ravine, into the widening valleys, across and under rotting logs, eating away at tiny rootlets and massive roots.

Inevitably, the ponds will fill again, sending the excess, the growing surplus, down the grass-filled spillways into the island lagoons and on into the new wetlands in the valley, marking with its own margins where the mature stage of the new marsh will be.

Eventually the creeks, after a long summer respite, will take over the job of moving it all into the Hocking, the broad Ohio, and wherever else it may be going.

That's quite a streak of hyperbole to be brought on by a meager little quarter-inch rain on this late morning in October. But, my friends and fellow countrymen, that's how I react when July thunderstorms move in a consistent pattern to the north or south away from wherever I may be.

My condition worsens in August. Weather maps make promises that they do not keep. Thermometers blow their tops. In an arid September I become irrational, moody, cynical, very poor company.

So, this sweet morning, this dawn with a wet face, this hour that just stepped out of a shower, may well be the cause of this unseemly spate of exuberant prose.

That's just the way it is. I simply can't do otherwise.

Autumn Stage Settings

MY FIREWOOD FOR ALL THE COMING WINTER months is now cut and split, hauled and stacked in rather neat order, I'm proud to say. Most of it is stored in the three places that need its promises of warmth—my house, my shop, and our family cabin. But at least two other generous supplies, probably for another winter to come, are neatly stored in the woodlots where they were sawed and readied for future use.

These cooling days of October lend anticipation to this annual chore. There's a feel-good element to the results— neat stacks of fuel for the fireplaces and heating stoves of December and January.

I went out into my nondescript backyard this morning to spread corn and sunflower seeds for my motley feathered clients. Nine trim wild turkeys promptly came trotting in to claim their share. An even larger flock of Canada geese was already on hand. They mixed with a hint of uncertain animosity—an air of unease. But this is a day for other outdoor dramas. A sharp change in temperature is evident. My old jacket wraps pleasantly across my shoulders. Great rafts of ballooning clouds sweep across a sky so blue I lack the exact adjectives to describe it.

Here in these foothills of the Appalachians, the low-forested ridges are dipping into remembered pots of color—hues and tints that only a rare artist could capture. A new stage setting is in place. Star-shaped leaves of sweet gum trees are sporting their favorite shades of maroon and purple, gold and sienna. Already the buckeyes and walnuts lift bare branches to trace dark lines on the sky canvas. Oaks, of course, are more stubborn, as are the young beech trees. Although the season has stolen their summer green, quite likely a few more weeks will pass before chill winds whirl the leaf harvest away into brown drifts in the wooded footlight recesses.

The two grizzled old groundhogs that have been regular customers at my backyard restaurant all summer are now in their annual hibernation under the foundation blocks of my house. I'll expect to see them again next February—and they'll be right hungry. When I last saw them several days ago their obesity was obvious.

Now, I admit to a certain amount of bias when it comes to the drama of season changes. Spring is wonderful. It's an awakening. Old aches tend to diminish. The first jonquil and the first tawny morel are causes for celebration. Swarms of warblers will move through the woodland edges and old ragged fencerows, their songs flawless. The white pines will light new candles on the tips of every branch.

But at this moment the third act is coming to a close. Someone left a backstage door open, and a chill breeze is making the audience restless. It's the cue for November to slip in and take a bow, but I'm still applauding the drama of Act II, when goldenrod and joe-pye weed were still saying good-bye to July and August. If I may be permitted to carry my metaphor just a bit farther, perhaps I'll leave before the final curtain comes down. I prefer comedy, ballet dancers, romantic interludes, and rollicking songs with easy-to-remember lyrics.

It is clear, then, that I plan to remove December, January and February from the calendars that are now arriving daily in my mail. But there *will* be March again, and there *will* be April. It's a promise—a pledge. I have paid for my ticket at the box office down at the end of my lane, and I plan to be on time to claim my center-row seat when the curtain goes up again next April.

Invocation

Touch me, gently,
Here and here again
With fingers soft
As thistle down
Or autumn winds.
Let your warm breath
Remind me of my Aprils,
For this is now November
And I can feel the frost.

White-Throated Sparrow

I TRY TO AVOID A MIRROR WHENEVER POSSIBLE. Mirrors are simply too truthful, too accurate in reflecting the reality of my passing years.

Apparently I did not do a careful job of shaving the grizzled stubble from my chin this morning. A few unkempt patches appear here and there. They most certainly will grow more obvious as the day wears on.

My wood-carving activities early this morning have left a trail of sawdust and chips not only around the old rocking chair in my workshop, but also up and down the front of the sweater that I unwisely put on at daybreak. Wool sweaters have an amazing ability to capture wood shavings and sawdust, not to mention spiderwebs and undetected dust from old shelves clinging to surrounding walls.

My favorite wood chisel needed sharpening—a fifteen-minute task involving a brief use of an emery wheel, a touch-up with a fine-grooved file, and a careful polishing of the razorlike blade on a well-worn finishing stone.

Now I have an accumulation of evidence on the front of my jeans—several drops of lubricating oil as well as tiny flecks of metal that will become embedded and hard to remove.

I've been down this road before. Spending endless hours carving basswood and water tupelo into wrens and robins leaves rather obvious trails. There by the old band saw is an ancient basket slowly filling with bits and pieces cut from along the pattern outlines.

Long ago I gave up keeping score. The soft gleam of a finished wing feather on a scarlet tanager or a Baltimore oriole seems far more important than the long, long hours spent with carving knives and tiny brushes dripping across my smeared old painting table. (Or worrying about my beard stubble, for that matter.)

Here at my elbow sits yesterday's bird—a white-throated sparrow. It is not a masterpiece designed to bring a record price from some famous collector. Yet it pleases me in so many ways.

I recall my very first view of a whitethroat. Both of us—this lovely bird and I—were exploring the edges of a tangled thicket far down in the Appalachian hills of eastern Kentucky. Even as a rank amateur bird watcher, I had no difficulty recognizing this sparrow with brilliant patches of yellow in front of its dark eyes.

Now more than three-quarters of a century later, the white-throated sparrow that comes now and then to explore my backyard may be en route to Lake Erie or a familiar thicket on this old farm of mine.

As they move north in April or come wandering back south in September's fading days, I'll try to remember to roll out a clean welcome mat and scatter some extra seed along the edges of their favorite thickets.

And, of course, more often than not, I may enjoy the amazing varieties of other members of the sparrow family that bless this entire North American continent of ours.

Whether they wear white or golden crowns, sport black throats or black chins, are clay-colored or rufous-winged, they are an amazing family. My crummy old field guide lists twenty-nine varieties. Seven of them were named for the ornithologists who claimed to have first identified them.

Their sizes range from the seven-inch-long white-crowneds to the tiny five-inch black-chinned variety of our great Southwest.

I love them all, even the house sparrow, which followed our own ancestors from Europe more than a century ago. They are welcome in my backyard. However, they obviously prefer my neighbor's horse barn and feedlot. They're truly tough little birds.

November's End

THIS IS THE LAST DAY OF A LOVELY NOVEMBER. It matters not one bit that the morning weatherman, in doleful terms, painted a dismal picture of blizzard conditions sweeping across the mountain passes of Montana and Wyoming, threatening to stir up the already turbulent waters of Lakes Superior, Michigan, and Erie.

No, here in my little valley, here on my own old farm that a friend calls "el Paraiso," it is the nearest thing to spring. Really!

My thermometer, the one that sticks its toes outdoors, registers forty-six degrees. The pond surface is a dark mirror. Bare branches of the nearby trees—cypress from the southland sharing space with my native ashes and maples—show no hint of air movement.

Yet low-hanging clouds, torn into long gray banners, are moving eastward like a host of marathon runners at the start of a race, eager, fresh, filled with the adrenaline of April.

Sometime in the night hours more rain has slipped in over the western ridges. It's a wet world out there. The long, long spillway from the pond, bone dry through August and an almost perfect September, glitters now with overflow. The pond no longer is thirsty.

Out in my ragged backyard a lone wild goose, unable to fly because of an injured wing, waits for me to serve up breakfast. His family and friends come shouting in from down valley to stage their daily repertoire of mock chases and political debates over who gets the last grains of corn, which I am obligated to provide as my ticket for the show.

Southeast, over the crowns of the taller pines, there's a hint of sun. It etches the cloud bank, making the nearer masses even darker. Suddenly, however, there is a downpour. The pond surface is shattered. Rain washes the windows of my little room cleaner, certainly, than they need to be.

And then it is over. The floodlights of late morning come up. Within minutes the entire cloud bank, no longer dark and threatening, sweeps off to the east, now backlit by the sun coming up from somewhere down south, and the trailing clouds take on a billowing whiteness, a cottony softness.

Everything is squeaky clean: the pale green of the old lawn, the weathered clumps of pampas grasses along the face of the dam, the scattered leaves stripped from the clump of sweet bay magnolia at the corner of my house.

In my tiny greenhouse, heated only by the sun, spikes of crocus and grape hyacinths already are poking up through the soil in pots that I filled just days ago. Obviously they, too, agree with me that this must be April.

This surely is the sea change, the long-predicted global warming trend, when Januarys and Februarys will be relegated to the history books. We will sit on shaded park benches and tell our unbelieving grandchildren about the olden days when snow piled high against the doors of home, when blizzard winds whipped drifts across the river and through the woods to grandmother's house where, naturally, we always went by horse-drawn sleigh.

Didn't we?

Autumn's Encore

Fall still is sharing center stage
Loving the full applause,
Taking an encore as a just reward
For playing out its role beyond its time

While winter, in the wings,
Waits for its cue.

Winter

December Snow

Gently they came,
Those sky petals of snow,
Soft, soft like the purring of kittens.
They brushed the needles
Of pine, of hemlocks,
With gentle paws,
With curled whiskers.
Pin oaks tasted the
Flakes on twig tips,
Savoring cool flavors,
Ephemeral, effervescent.

Juncos matched breast feathers
With white driftings,
Then left no tracing.
The curtains of day
Closed with no fanfare,
Not even a wind whisper.

My Backyard Adventures

AT TIMES THERE SEEMS TO BE A HINT OF SKEPTICISM in the way some of my friends look at me when I breathlessly talk about my backyard adventures with local wildlife or nature in general.

For instance, I often comment on such things as the bachelor life of the four elegant tom turkeys that come loping down from the nearby wooded ridge each morning, when I go outside to spread corn across the open slope. These old bearded birds are more obviously confident than the great flock of sleek young ones that follow their mother hens into my generous feedlot once or twice each week. Their nervous attitude will change with time, as they learn that my old farm is a security zone, complete with breakfast.

On the other hand, I'm also a pushover for things that are more permanent than turkeys. Two young cypress trees brace themselves at the edge of my pond, just about thirty feet from my front door. They are not yet thirty years old, but their muscular trunks already measure at least two feet in diameter. Their massive roots have sent up several gnarled "knees" in the surrounding lawn and in the shallow waters of the spillway.

These trees are not native here, yet it is obvious that they are adapting as well to southern Ohio as they do to South Carolina. Often I dream of how big they may be when my great grandsons relax in their shade a half century down the road. Today they stand like freshly signed promissory notes.

This morning as I came up the river valley, well over three hundred Canada geese caused me to pull my car over to the roadside for a few moments of contemplation. There they were, resting in the winter sun and grazing on the greensward that had been kept neat and trim all summer by the river conservancy crew. Should I be surprised that, unlike their ancestors of less than half a century ago, they no longer fly south under November skies to winter in the bayous of Louisiana or the valley of the Rio Grande? I don't think so.

Last evening I sat in my little sunroom, turning the early chapter pages of James Herriot's newest book, *Every Living Thing*. It was quiet time.

I glanced up as a great ball of white rolled across the outside deck, following the base of my windows. It was a skunk! But what a specimen! Almost completely white and fully furred for the winter climate, here was one spectacular animal. It moved around with casual ease searching for food scraps or sunflower seeds along the base of the railing, where I spread such holiday cheer for cardinals and chickadees, titmice and mourning doves.

Now, as my pen moves across the pages of my journal, I am interrupted by the sunlit flash of a young white-tailed buck hurrying across the east lawn and into the woodland. I wonder what's the hurry. Is he following a late-blooming, reluctant doe?

With midwinter at hand, passion time is over, fellow. All those sleek and willing does should be satisfied by now, preparing for the delivery of new fawns in late April and the early days of May.

As I swivel my old chair around to scan the bird-feeding platform again, a muskrat emerges from a hole in the pond ice and scrambles up the bank, searching for seeds that may have been scattered by the ever-hungry cardinals and jays.

This has been a good day—a very good winter day. But now, only the crowns of the tall pines across the ridge still catch the golden rays from the western sky. The white icing of my pond is in shadow. Like the hands of a compass, the taller trees cast sharp lines to the east. Ground shadows are deepening. There is no birdsong, no sweep of wind now.

My cat is asleep on the rug at my feet, perhaps dreaming of the field mouse it caught this morning in the tall grass down along the lane.

As this day winds down, I wonder whether there may be a few tasty leftovers that can be rescued from my old refrigerator and turned into a gourmet dinner. I doubt it, but it's worth trying. All this talk makes an old man hungry. Good night, y'all.

Ring In the New

DECEMBER HAS RUN ITS COURSE. THESE WINTER weeks have brought their light snow blankets on at least three occasions. I'm tempted to use milder adjectives to record the weather patterns that followed familiar roadways into our old Appalachians.

The ice cover on my nearby pond shines with a wet sheen of meltwater. A solid cloud cover has moved in from the northwest. The sun, which offered to warm my little valley early this morning, offers not even a hint of its westerly location now in midafternoon.

My calendar reminds me, of course, that this *is* a new year. It *is* January one, delivered all wrapped in ribbons and tinsel and filled with promises. As a dyed-in-the-wool optimist, I fully expect that most of those promises will be kept.

Let me list a few certainties.

At this moment the usual gaggle of geese, twenty or more, stand idly on the old worn lawn and on the ice-covered pond. They, together with a few crows, have cleaned up most of the shelled corn that I spread earlier, at their request. I can assure you that when March comes blustering in to my little valley, only two of these geese will remain.

That pair will have seniority—and they will readily enforce it. This pond is their nursery. It was eleven years ago when they raised their first brood here, and their lease is still in force, their rent paid in full. I'm a satisfied landlord.

Four sleek tom turkeys, dressed in iridescent bronze and gold, are coming down the nearby ridge at this moment. This is their feedlot, too. Like bachelors at a local beer joint, they will avoid the numerous hens that claim these same hills and briar patches until spring arrives with a truckload of hormone stimulants.

Then every day will be showtime. Great fantails will spread. Wings will swing like Main Street awnings. Their featherless heads will become chalk white, their throats blood red. It will be mating time, and don't you forget it, all you hen turkeys of the neighborhood.

Right now the pair of old groundhogs are still sound asleep under the foundation of my house. Hibernation, it's called. But come February second or thereabout, they, too, will roll over in bed, look at the calendar, and decide it's time to rise and shine. Reluctantly, of course, judging by their somewhat disheveled appearance after several weeks of bedtime, they will crawl out to reconnoiter the neighborhood.

The pair of barred owls that for several years has claimed a spacious cavity in an old maple tree down toward the main creek will be nesting again when March comes in like a lion—or a lamb. They will notify me when family time arrives, because this is a very vocal pair. Their *whoo-whoo-whooing* calls will bounce back and forth well into midsummer.

By late March, when tempting morels are pushing up through the leaf mold, when trillium and pale violets add color to the winter-worn palette, I'll walk softly down along the marshes and vernal pools to listen for the chorus of spring peepers and the coughing calls of green frogs. I'll be anxious to find clusters of maroon bells opening on the pawpaw trees along the margins of my old fields. Sweet sap will be flowing in the gnarled old sugar maple trees, and our resident sapsuckers will know it's time to open new rows of holes in the gray bark to serve as tiny fountains.

Morning after morning, soft blankets of fog will fill my little valley. Birdsong will be soft and infrequent until April and May schedule a full round of rehearsals. By January's reluctant end, I know there will be great maroon blooms of skunk cabbage pushing up through the tangled marsh that has slowly, slowly developed below the face of my oldest man-made pond. Not until late April will the great fan leaves of this strange native be dominant among the clumps of lizard tail.

Last autumn, after a wet, wet summer, new colonies of water lilies were apparent here and there in the pond shallows. The floating seeds explore new homesites, transported by winds and mild currents. When another midsummer prompts them to open great pink blooms on the water surface, I'll be reminded of the few ragged plants that I salvaged from older marshes among these beloved hills and valleys and forced their roots into new lodgings in my neighborhood. Obviously, they didn't mind.

So go my wandering thoughts this midmorning of a fresh new year. I feel no guilt for introducing newcomers to this ever-changing haven of mine. Two robust Labrador spruce grow in a pair of open spaces here outside my window. Clumps of giant pampas grass stand tall across the ridge of the dam. Someday, in some far-off year, the pair of bald cypress trees by the spillway will rival their Everglade ancestors in size. Measuring changes in the natural world is hardly a precise science.

But the joy is in the result itself. Already, beyond a doubt, this is a very fine new year, at least as measured by my own choices of rules.

What's your yardstick?

The "Old" Year

This has been a fine year,
Filtered through foggy mornings,
Burnished by sun polish,
Wrapped in the cold light
Of gibbous moons.
Hummingbirds have found nectar
In its June hours.
Wrens have nested
In its hair.
Dragonflies and monarchs,
Spring peepers and deermice
Danced to its rhythms,
Hummed its melodies,
So old, so new.
Gently its days rest in my wrinkled hands.

Hill Country Streams

A HALF-MILE STRETCH OF MARGARET CREEK wanders across the eastern acres of this old farm, following a serpentine channel that seems aimless. Coming down the ancient valley that was the home of a bustling coal-mining community more than a century ago, the erratic current has cut deeply into the floodplain, twisting and turning around the roots of riverine sycamores, willows, and soft maples, and old sandstone rocks cut from the feet of nearby hills.

It is, not surprisingly, a restless stream. It wanders. It responds to spring thunderstorms, of course, and winter floods, by exploring possible new channels. Overflowing its banks, as happens at least once each year, it washes over the old valley floor, layering last summer's weed-fields and leaving vernal pools along the path that it obviously followed, and deserted, several centuries ago.

Generations of salamanders and peeper frogs come by in early spring to start new nurseries. Minnows explore the changeable pools, darting in and out of sun and shadow with the effect of fireflies on June evenings.

Families of beavers, absent for at least a century, again can choose the trees that they may decide to harvest. I do not always agree with their decisions. Within the past twelve months they have girdled and killed three fine black oaks, one of them quite likely a century or more old. It still stands, resisting decay, its roots exposed in the cutbank above the creek bed. These old veterans of the valley may be my choices for next winter's firewood.

This deeply cut channel, with its erratic and voluminous floodwaters, does not fit the dam-building engineering plans of beaver families. They prefer wooded valleys and gentle currents. They can adapt quite well, however. Here they dig dens in the steep banks, homesites that suffer only minor damage from spring floods and to which the old flat-tailed owners can return when the currents calm down and resume their placid gurgles.

Wood ducks return home here each March and April from winter vacations along the bayous and lazy stream valleys of the Gulf states. They may prefer a nesting site in the hollow trunk of a streamside sycamore, but such prefab homes are not always available. More than once I have found them using cavities in old worn oaks and maples hundreds of yards from the pools and currents of the nearest streams. Within hours after hatching, the tiny, downy youngsters flutter recklessly from their high nurseries, bouncing like rubber balls on limbs and ground hazards. Seldom injured, they follow the anxious, plaintive cries of their mothers, until they reach the relative safety of the creek waters.

Less than forty years ago the first graceful white-tailed deer came wandering back into this old valley where farming was slowly coming to an end. They decided to stay. Now their numbers are legion, their graceful presence a blessing.

Already in midwinter the bucks have shed their antlers, and by June new points will be growing between their always-alert ears—points that will be sheathed in velvet until the first frosts of September.

I mark all these changes in the cycle of seasons, in the constant regeneration of ridges and valleys, with mild amazement.

From my earliest teens I had a penchant for wandering the margins of hill country streams, yet not until the late 1940s did the lovely wood duck return from the edge of extinction to reclaim its heritage and reward my curiosity.

Now, in these old hills, the roles are reversed for bobwhites, ruffed grouse, and cottontail rabbits. I am unsure of the reasons for their relative absence. Yet blessings still abound. Pessimism has no place here. I have trails to wander, slowly, along wooded ridges that were cut more than half a century ago. Gentle currents whisper over sandbars and around the twisting contours of Margaret Creek as it wanders through my farm.

I cry a little when windstorms blow down old fencerow trees whose growth rings measure years beyond memory. Yet my smile spans a mile when I stop to measure the robust waistline of impressive giants that I planted here less than half a century past.

This, too, will be a fine year, friends: a very fine year. Take my word for it.

Visitors in the Snow

FOR AN OLD BIRD WATCHER LIKE ME, THIS HAS been a red-letter occasion, a day to celebrate and re-member. No, there has been no visit by a snowy owl out of the Arctic tundra; no red crossbills have been working the tops of my evergreens. I'm still waiting for a visit by a greedy little flock of evening grosbeaks.

Not a single "life" bird has come to call. But I'll re-member this day for many a season and many a reason, all because of the sheer volume of avian visitors.

A four-inch blanket of snow was draped snugly over my low, rugged old hills and weedfields several days ago, making life difficult for those feathered friends of mine that depend on the seeds of foxtail, stick-tights, long-faded Michaelmas daisies, and bull thistle. A week of unrelenting cold locked the wild smorgasbord up tight.

Then sometime in the dark hours of last night, three more inches of white fluff covered the rumpled surface of old snow, giving every mound of earth and dense shrub a voluptuous look. But as the morning temperature edged slowly above the freezing point, a cold drizzle of rain materialized, turning the whiteness into a sodden mass with a crusty coating.

Shut off from every source of wild food, birds came to my feeders in growing numbers. By ten o'clock the first two quarts of sunflower seeds and a quart of cracked corn had disappeared. There were juncos by the dozens. Titmice and chickadees darted from here to over there. Blue jays brought their relatives. Song and white-throated sparrows came out of the nearby thickets. At one point I surveyed the cardinals—there were no less than thirty-three moving in for their share. A pair of Carolina wrens tested the menu. Downy, hairy, and red-bellied woodpeckers stood in line at the suet feeder. Mourning doves were everywhere.

Then, incredibly, the scene changed. A flock of at least a thousand grackles moved in and took over. The view from my window not more than ten feet away was astounding. Like the dark funnel of a winged tornado they whirled and dipped, commandeering every inch of space where I had spread a new banquet. Within five minutes the table was bare.

Despite the bravery of the mob, there were a lot of nervous Nellies flashing away into the nearby trees each time I moved even slightly indoors. However, their return was prompt. These birds were hungry!

Twice more I refilled the feeders and scattered grain and seeds on the deck railing. Each time they cleared it away in minutes.

Suddenly it all changed again. A Cooper's hawk rocketed into the scene from the nearby woods. With a literal roar of wings, the grackles left even more suddenly than they had come. Like a formless amoeba, like a dark puff of coal smoke, they whirled away down the hollow, chased by a predator that couldn't select a victim.

Now all my old displaced neighbors are back. Although my little backyard looks like a chicken feedlot, the icy snow dirtied with seed hulls and droppings, the cardinals and juncos don't mind. They find it easier to share the bounty with a mixed crowd of chickadees, sparrows, and jays than with a mob of black-robed grackles.

A single red-winged blackbird has just arrived. What's he doing this far north in January, for Pete's sake?

Overture

Tonight the west wind blew out all its candles,
The season came of age. The last leaf fell
And lodged alee a gray encrusted stone.

Now winter waits just over yonder ridge
With new designs in frosted crystal.

The firewood stands in regimented lines
Uncalled, as yet, to arms against the cold.

Bird-Watching Surprises

No BIRD-WATCHING FAME ATTACHES ITSELF TO these old hills in the southeastern corner of Ohio. It is that section of land where the Ohio River swings wide past the faces of little towns that remember great sternwheelers and the flow of muddy floodwaters in Februarys past.

Those who pack their binoculars and long-visored caps and go searching for north- or southbound migrants seldom knock on my door. I have no advertisements in bird-watching magazines promising a plethora of hummingbirds or the serenade of a wood thrush if you should come by for a visit.

In fact, I'll be glad to join you if perchance you are en route to Point Pelee, Ontario, some late April, when the warblers winnow down onto the welcoming north shore of Lake Erie.

Call me if you have space on your next trip to Hawk Mountain or Cape May or the rugged, lonely, barren ridges of Dolly Sods in the West Virginia mountains. I can always find time to scan the chill skies for a sight of a falcon or the powerful silhouette of a golden eagle riding the upwelling thermals.

But most of the time, season after season, the birds that call my backyard home are quite possibly the same familiar ones that come faithfully to your feeders and fledge their young in the nearby shrubbery.

Oh, but there are exceptions! The practice of bird watching seems to insist on springing surprises on even the most blasé of us. You want examples? One morning not so long ago, a Louisiana waterthrush came to call. Teetering politely as usual, it landed on the dock that extends from my deck out to the edge of my backyard pond. Less than twenty feet away from my sunroom where I sat savoring my second cup of coffee, this handsome little cousin of the warbler clan proceeded to explore the entire ten-foot dock, picking up bits of sunflower seed or some other avian tidbits that had scattered from the nearby feeder. A bit later it spent at least an hour patrolling the pond edges, certainly a more typical habitat than the dock.

I realize that a Louisiana waterthrush is not rare or endangered—just uncommon. I usually can find one or two each summer deep in some wooded hollow in our hill country, busily searching the edges of a clear little rocky stream.

Once, from the same sunroom vantage point, I watched in astonishment as a great blue heron came striding majestically along my deck. Suddenly it saw its reflection in the glass window. It shot upward. One wing, the one nearest the glass, was slowly raised to a completely upstretched position. The great bird marched sedately past the entire window area, then turned and, lowering one wing and raising the other, it retraced its solemn parade route. Obviously it liked what it saw—or seemed assured that it had impressed a rival. Without further ado, it returned to the pond edge to study the local menu.

A pair of barred owls resides in a cavity of an ancient sugar maple just down hollow from my home. There's nothing particularly unusual about that, I know. I have had barred owls as neighbors before. They are certainly interesting, easy to converse with at night, and always curious about who cooks for me, even though it is none of their owlish business.

But this pair seems unaware that they are night owls. All through late spring and early summer, at any convenient daylight hour, they *hoo-hooed,* they squalled, and seemed to engage in unseemly quarrels. At times it appeared they were on the verge of domestic violence. Surely I misinterpreted their motives.

Three pairs of Canada geese regularly nest at the ponds of my old hill farm. This has been going on for eight summers. I feed them well. I give them maximum security. I talk a reasonable version of goose language with them. We seem to be good neighbors.

Yet invariably, when the little yellow goslings are no more than two days old, the nervous parents proceed to lead their broods off across the overgrown weedfields to one of the other ponds. A day or two later they lead them back home, repeating this back-and-forth trek time after time until the youngsters actually are able to take flight.

As one might guess, this jittery conduct is hazardous. More than once over the years, one or more of the tiny goslings has become lost in the jungles of ragweed and goldenrod and was never seen again. Their parents, sadly enough to me, don't seem to notice the loss.

Purple martins frustrate me. They have done so throughout my long bird-loving years. They absolutely refuse to accept my hospitality. They have never, ever, nested in the homemade apartment condos or the fancy factory-made palaces that I have long maintained in areas that, experts tell me, are ideal for these impressive colonizers.

Yet, down the road a bit, at the edge of a busy parking lot at a little country restaurant, purple martins have a ball. They annually raise healthy, active, noisy broods of youngsters in an old metal house that has never been cleaned out by anyone—and is currently on the verge of falling apart. So what? To this family of martins it is home sweet home. But, not on my property.

I revel, though, in my little homegrown successes. Not so long ago, a lovely glossy ibis, with its gracefully curved bill, spent a day and a half picking its way around the edges of my little oxbow marsh. This is no small journey for a Florida native. Ohio is seldom on their travel schedule.

Earlier, when my little marsh was still brand new, it attracted a least bittern. After more than seven decades of birding nuttiness, this was a life first for me. Now, you'll agree, that is one long wait.

I don't really expect another surprise tomorrow. No sweat. There'll be the usual congregation of chickadees and cardinals, finches and jays, doves and blackbirds,

together with their motley friends, cleaning out my backyard feeders. My bill at the feed store will continue to
rival my grocery expenditures.

But, who knows, someday perhaps a keel-billed tou-
can or a motmot may come wandering up this way from
southern Mexico. I promise not to be too surprised.

Settling In

Early afternoon, and the wind has swung around from almost due north. The gusts shatter the snowflakes into fragments, blurring the far side of the valley into grayness.

When the velocity increased suddenly about an hour earlier, the old white pines across the pond lost their packs of snow in an instant, creating a whiteout that completely hid the ridgeline and the dark, perpendicular pattern of tree trunks beyond the near edge. If the wind continues its vigorous swirling dance, it is unlikely that a new snow cover will build again on the needle clusters or the starkly bare tree limbs.

The storm that came out way in the dark hours of last night, mounding up to at least eight inches on protected flat surfaces, was otherwise well behaved. I found no pile-up of wind-driven mounds. I heard no moaning in the house eaves; no whipping of branches in the ash tree near my bedroom window.

In the early morning I got up to study the transformation. The whiteness enhanced the diffused moonlight;

cloudcover reflected the lights from town far down the valley.

I watched an opossum wandering around in the deep snow, probably looking for food scraps that I had thrown out for just such night visitors. It gave the appearance of a soccer ball rolling around in the semidarkness. Later in the day I examined its trail. The tracks were partially covered, but the continuous line left by its dragging bare tail was clearly visible.

This day, with all other avian restaurants shut down by the smothering snowpack, birds come to my feeders in flocks. I count them over and over and average the numbers to determine a semiaccurate total.

Juncos come in force, at least thirty, working their preferred low feeding areas, picking daintily and politely for the smallest scraps of cracked corn and sunflower seed. Only occasionally will one patiently work a larger bit of corn around in its small bill until it can be reduced to swallowing size.

Mourning doves, more than twenty, follow a predictable regular pattern of visits. Within a matter of minutes the entire flock will come down out of the nearby trees, their wings whistling musically, landing on top of the spread grain and seed. They gorge, swallowing sunflower and cracked corn without hesitation. Ten minutes later, their crops bulging, they fly off to a nearby favorite tree, sitting undisturbed and unruffled for the next hour or so while their gizzards and digestive tract do their assigned chores. Then, with clockwork regularity, the flock returns for another session in their favorite cafeteria line.

I'm glad to see the house finches return this winter. The peak population of two or three years ago was decimated by an eye disease, which wiped out hundreds—even thousands—of these lovely birds. The females and juveniles are marked with all-over dark stripes, the males duded up in crowns and breasts of soft crimson. Now they come to the feeders in small, well-organized flocks, eating rather companionably with their kin and the other hungry, if more erratic, visitors. Chickadees and titmice are everywhere, but are almost impossible to count. I can only estimate—there must be dozens. They flit down, look over the table for one brief moment, select a sunflower seed and fly off to some favorite perch where they hold down the seed and peck away at the husk until the kernel is exposed. Then it's back for another—and another.

Cardinals, certainly no fewer than twenty today, are more methodical. They prefer to remain undisturbed while selecting a grain or seed that they grind with their stout orange-yellow bills until the edible portion can be swallowed. Usually there is nothing hurried about their table manners.

Six or eight blue jays are among my clients, but their feeding habits are anything but regular. They fly in aggressively, one after another, scare off more timid visitors, gulp down a dozen or more seeds, and it's off and away again. But they'll be back.

A few song and white-throated sparrows come quietly, foraging for bits of grain and seed at ground level. Their lovely, subtle feather pattern causes me to automatically reach for the binoculars one more time.

The pair of resident Carolina wrens comes by now and then, searching in familiar crannies for dormant spiders and insect egg clusters. They may occasionally pick up tiny grain bits, but this is not their cup of tea. Always independent souls, they show no sociability toward my other avian visitors.

The usual contingent of downy, hairy, and red-bellied woodpeckers comes and goes, from the suet feeders hanging on the pond-side ash tree to the peanut butter log in the sweet bay magnolia, and momentarily to the tray of sunflower seeds.

Now and then I watch the acrobatics of the overwintering white-breasted nuthatches and brown creepers as they hitch up and down the suet feeder tree.

So go my hours, this mid-January day. As I finish these lines, the clouds have moved on over the eastern hills. Fluffs of cotton batting follow across a sky that reminds me of the blue of a nest full of robin eggs. The sun is warming, but the shadows it casts have brittle edges. Chill wind gusts remind me to throw another log on the fire.

A good time to read, with my feet comfortably exposed to the flickering flames.

Winter's Serenade

Today brought wren song
Out of the snow
Across the wind
Bright as the spot of light on eye
Sharp as the edge of ice on eave
Rhythm as right as the moment.

My heart sang its own song
Out of the snow
Across the wind.

Did you catch the melody?

The Long Cold

THIS IS A WINTER OF THE LONG COLD, THE GRAY sky. The pond is armored in ice as thick as bridge timbers, softened only in appearance by inches of snow so airy that each flake rests lightly against its neighbors. Seemingly weightless, it molds the stiff cones of the pair of Labrador spruce that stand guard outside my window.

Day after day, the temperature range, too, has been frozen—zero to ten in the mornings, mid-twenties at midday. My thermometer that timidly holds a tiny vial of mercury against the outside wall has forgotten how to count above twenty-eight degrees.

Across the little valley, where the dark trunks of pines draw pencil-straight perpendicular lines against the white curve of the ridge, rhododendron bushes huddle in semi-hibernation. Their black-green leaves hang curled like old candles with flames snuffed out. There are buds that stand upright at the end of stout branches, promising explosions of pink and white next May and early June. They test my patience sorely.

In reality, however, I seem to be as sedentary as the morning scenery. My few red corpuscles are shuffling along at a leisurely pace, nudged a bit perhaps by two cups of steaming coffee.

But there's no lack of frenetic activity. Juncos are here by the dozens, picking through the layers of seed hulls for tiny bits of kernels scattered unintentionally by cardinals and white-throated and song sparrows. There is no such thing as an inactive junco. One second in a single spot is ample. They twitch. Their white outer tail feathers fan in millisecond bursts.

More than two months will blow by before the migratory urge will remind them that honeymoons are to be spent in the far north woods, so I doubt that the drab little females even notice as yet how handsome the males are with their dark heads, slate gray backs, and bellies white as the drifts on which they are wading at this moment.

I'm not really very reliable as a census taker. It is obvious that the cast of feathered characters in this daily performance is both varied and numerous. Half a dozen white-throated sparrows mingle with scores of house finches at the buffet. Their colors and markings are muted. Even the ones that appear to be adult males have yet to dress up for spring romancing.

A single Carolina wren comes by momentarily, sampling the peanut butter and suet supply somewhat reluctantly. Their preferred diet of dormant insects and egg cases is well hidden by the snow.

Chickadees and titmice come and go with the regularity of metronomes. Three song sparrows wander in and eat quietly, unobtrusively, as if hoping to go unnoticed.

Six jays, acting like hyped-up athletes ready for any game, muscle their way to the trays, eat with poor manners for a few short minutes, then fly off as if to see what's going on in the next block.

Unexpectedly, as I watch my hungry flocks, two young white-tailed deer come trotting across the ice, leaving necklaces of dainty hoofprints cut sharply into the snow. They paw around the base of the main feeder, uncovering grain and seeds overlooked by the birds. Short yearlings from last April, they quite probably are orphans. One of my young neighbors excitedly told of shooting a mature doe during the recent gun season. He said that two smaller deer had accompanied her. A large pool of scarlet marked where she had fallen just beyond my fenceline.

Although I fully understand the excitement of hunting and the essential role that animals, wild and otherwise, have played down through millennia in the proclaimed advancement of humankind, the accumulation of my own years has altered my perspective considerably. My guns are quiet under a quarter-century coating of dust.

Admittedly, I'm now an old softy. The squirrels efficiently cleaning out the feeders on my deck are only mildly and momentarily alert when I step outside. The vibrations of my footsteps are no disturbance to the fat groundhog in winter sleep under the house foundation.

Now and then I scatter a few gallons of corn down along the river where a great flock of Canada geese spends part of the winter on the open water below White's Mill or grazing on the frozen grasses above the channel banks. A few days ago I had a bonus, when a trio of herring gulls, driven downstate from the frozen waters of Lake Erie, cruised gracefully up and down the Hocking River, looking for an easy lunch along the littered shoreline. A frozen carp would do quite nicely, I'm sure.

And so it goes. The long gray days will stretch far on into the new year. Almost unnoticed, the daylight will arrive a few precious moments earlier each morning, warming my old bones a degree or two. The sun, when it reluctantly comes up across the gray silhouette of my old hometown half a mile away, will most certainly be moving a few centimeters farther north each circle of day.

It would be easy, perhaps, to face each day reluctantly, harboring melancholy impulses as being my due. It really is not easy for an old man to appreciate the pleasure that handsome young forecasters seem to derive from their predictions of cold fronts and blinding blizzards sweeping down the east face of the Rockies and up across the Great Plains into my backyard.

But time's in short supply. There's a hungry chickadee just outside my window. A pale ray of sunshine has just broken through the leaden clouds over east, falsely promising a heat wave. I need to bring in another load of wood for my evening fire—wood that was cut and split in the hot and sweaty days of last summer.

It is January. I barely have time to notice.

Do-Nothing Day

THIS IS AN EXCELLENT "DO-NOTHING" MORNING. At 9:30 my second cup of coffee fulfills my inner needs. The book I am reading is the kind that tolerates, even encourages, intermittent interruptions. Its title is *Free Wheeling,* and it is a staccato recording of a bicycle trip across America, west to east. I am now in the drier areas of eastern Oregon, nearing Idaho. The author, Richard Lovett, had just suffered a badly skinned elbow and two broken wheel spokes from a fall caused by his viewing of the far-off mountain scenery instead of a close-up view of the highway shoulder on which he was riding.

I understand. I've been through that wonder world a couple of times, by car, in years past. It's easy to be diverted by blue vistas and rocky canyons, or by the sight of a great golden eagle making majestic circles along the face of the sculptured range of dry mountains.

But I have no desire to indulge in memories right now. Like everyone else from Pomeroy to Penobscot, I am a reluctant but resigned prisoner of the elements.

Any description of the deep snow blanket that wraps up my little hollow would be filled with overused adjectives duplicated in weather reports and news stories from Buffalo to Boston.

It is just as well, for I'm satisfied by smaller, though far from mundane, things. At this moment a Carolina wren, its tail erect, its body feathers fluffed to harbor warmth, is busy at my doorsteps, sampling the handful of cookie crumbs that I tossed out just moments ago.

It would no doubt prefer to find a few hibernating spiders or neat packages of dormant insect larvae, but in mid-February the menu choices for resident wrens is somewhat limited.

A bit earlier this morning three Canada geese, obviously familiar with the local scene, circled my frozen, snowbound pond and came in for an easy landing on the deep white blanket. They were hungry. However, they were somewhat skittish, having avoided my home pond for almost a month because it had been frozen over. Within minutes they decided that conditions were too uncertain, and with a small chorus of honks they took off for the more open river valley down east. As February drags its reluctant feet through the calendar, I urge it on. March, I reason, may come on like a lion, with wind gusts that prune the dead limbs from my woodlots or fill my little valleys with boisterous storm water, but at least I will know that winter is on its way out of here. And not one day too soon.

This Land and I

MY THOUGHTS WANDER ALONG UNCHARTED PATHS this mid-February morning. They follow worn ridges where sassafras and dogwood mark the long-forgotten line of an ancient fence, or perhaps a path cows once traced to the sagging old barn for milking.

Like the eroded ravine that has forgotten its origin, I feel the wash of time in my own halting gait, in the extra care with which I step across the flat shale-stones and the exposed roots of trees that seem determined to reclaim their heritage.

This old worn land and I seem to be heading toward completely opposite destinations, but we follow the same well-drawn map. It is marked with remnant stumps, where old woodlands once grew. I can read the slope of a ridge where more than one farmer once cradled his meager stand of oats, or mowed an old hayfield with its sparse cover of red clover and timothy.

I climb over the corner post of the sagging wire fence and move along the path shaded by the grove of great white pines. They are less than half my years, yet their girth far exceeds my embrace. Their top candles reach at least a hundred feet toward the February clouds. I rest my sloping shoulder against the scaly bark and listen.

It was another spring when I tucked hundreds of those little pine seedlings across this slope—a spring when my load was light and my step was strong.

Turning down east, I follow the lane that leads to a weathered welcome sign. Windfall Ridge, it reads, named for the original orchard that marked these sparse acres. This is where my Harriet, as a child, wandered among the trees salvaging early ripened Jonathans and Winesaps, Rome Beauties and Grimes Goldens that had fallen in the wake of early autumn winds.

All those old apple trees are gone now, for their lifespan seldom marks half a century. The slowly decaying trunk of the last one lies along the path that once led to the barn that sheltered the family cows during winter storms. The hayloft rafters and eaves above made home space for phoebes, barn swallows, and Carolina wrens.

The paper nests of wasps were tucked here and there along the dusty, web-covered rafters. One summer the great globe of a nest of hornets echoed to a warning hum from the overhanging eaves.

July storms, however, create drama of their own. One late afternoon, under a dark cloud cover from somewhere west, the old structure came down. There it lay, along with the bent and twisted panels of metal roofing. A few of the foundation stones remain. Quite probably they remember that day—that hour.

Slowly, slowly I climb the nearby ridge. A truly ancient white oak marks where, more than a century ago, some former owner of this land set a fenceline and stapled barbed wires to that old tree trunk.

I lean against its massive, fluted trunk. I gaze skyward into its muscular limbs reaching out for their share of sunlight and ponder our parallel years. There is no morbidity in my contemplation of our shared century. The roots of this old *Quercus alba* have sunk deeply here, probing well beyond the dripline of its outreaching twigs.

By contrast, I have enjoyed a wanderlust that has led me to the vistas of Alaska, the plains of Kenya, and the willow-covered dikes of Holland.

Generations of robins have nested in the arms of that old oak of mine. Crows have called from its crown. White-tailed fawns have lain in its dappled shade.

A swing of twisted rope hangs down from a reaching arm. I hung it there—how many years ago—for my grandchildren—for my great-grandchildren. If my good fortune holds for another summer, perhaps I may watch their pendulum swing and hear their joyful cries again—and again.

This story, quite obviously, has no ending. There is sweetness to life that mixes its chemistry with tiny touches of bitterness. Years soften the razor-sharp edges of our days. There most certainly will be bright mornings—tomorrow and tomorrow.

Then I will wander again—even if only among my memories—where thrushes call and trillium blooms, and perhaps a lovely woman will touch my hand and steady my steps a bit.

Suddenly It's Spring!

Now, i know full well that the weather and I are gambling on an obviously premature announcement. March (even April) may yet lock up the pond under ice windows. I will not promise to like it, but the old pine trees across the way may have to shoulder another snow pack before it's time to welcome blooms of trillium and bloodroot.

Oh, there surely will be hoarfrost. The thermometer on my kitchen wall will register downscale from thirty-two degrees in the aftermath of lashing March winds. I promise to cross my fingers to protect the bloom on my grapevines and my lone dwarf apple tree, which is nearing fruit-bearing maturity out near my shop.

Yet surely it *is* spring. The signs are infallible.

Last week three lesser scaup, a drake and two hens, all dressed in resplendent breeding plumage acquired quite probably in the bayou country of Louisiana, dropped in for rest and refreshment at the big pond over in the middle of the farm. For two days they demonstrated their expertise at diving for whatever delicacies the old pond had to offer. In between their underwater exercises, they dozed in the little shaded backwaters, heads tucked snugly into their wing shoulders.

And then they were gone. The potholes and lake country of the Dakotas and maybe Saskatchewan were calling. They obviously felt the pull of ice-out time way up north.

But there are other signs, other reliable witnesses to this change of seasons. There's a fresh, clean quality to the air. Since midmonth two overly generous periods of rain have washed these old hills. Every breath drawn into my old lungs is an elixir. I walk the trails with just a whit more steadiness, a surge of energy that I have missed since the halcyon days of last October.

The greening sod, soaked to pillow softness, accepts my footprints with assurance that in days they will matter not at all.

Down along the brim-full marsh yesterday, I sat and watched a muskrat maneuver here and there among the emergent vegetation, pausing from time to time to sample something green and tasty.

For the first time this month, the peeper frogs were singing full chorus. I'm always surprised at the shrill quality of their mating calls. It is a sharp, piercing sound, especially when I stand by the shallow edge of the marsh for long moments until the entire colony, momentarily quieted by my arrival, resumes its amorous harmony.

Around a bend of the island pond I startled a pied-billed grebe. It dove with amazing suddenness, but the water is sufficiently clear and shallow that I could watch its passage along the narrow channels, where bluegills and fathead minnows are featured on grebe menus.

At seven this morning I opened the backdoor to relish the fifty-degree temperature. Even that slight sound and movement startled a pair of wood ducks into flight from up near the pond's western edge. These, too, are first of the season. Their plaintive cries trail down valley as they maneuver along the woodland overhang and disappear eastward like dark projectiles.

They'll come back. Quite probably they are natives returning to home territory. If so, they will remember exactly where I scatter generous helpings of corn all spring, all summer, and well into autumn, when the first big chill sends them into migration again.

The resident geese are back. These birds have completely forgotten the route to Texas and Mexico. All winter long, impervious to ice and snow, more than two hundred of the big Canadas have moved up and down the river valley, grazing for hours along the high ground of the open channel, where frequent mowing by the conservancy staff tends to keep the grass a bit greener in cold Decembers and Januarys.

Now, within the past two weeks, the big flock of more than two hundred massive birds has begun to peel apart. The older pairs, followed by their full-grown families of last season, are moving back home. They are almost defiantly territorial. The old pair that nests in an elevated box in the bay of my home pond returned five days ago. Several times already the goose has reexamined the nesting site where she has hatched families of downy yellow goslings each spring for the last seven years. Noisy courting rituals between the veteran lovers occur several times daily. Soon, when actual mating and egg-laying time arrives, the young members of the flock will find, to their unpleasant surprise, that they are no longer welcome in the neighborhood. Time after time the old gander will launch aggressive attacks on the siblings, finally driving them away from this familiar home valley.

That's life for a young goose. They soon learn to rejoin the familiar flock of other juveniles, all probably less than four years old, and will spend the summer months trading back and forth along the Hocking River and the nearby larger lakes and pocket marshes. Peace for all will return when the young of this coming summer graduate from flight school.

Any day now the little flocks of juncos and white-throated sparrows will suddenly disappear from beneath my backyard feeders. There's no announcement. One day they are here, the next they are gone—off to their summer homes in some far northern forests of Michigan and Wisconsin, Minnesota or Ontario. This morning, at feeding time, I reminded them to come back next fall—and bring the kids.

Mourning doves are becoming impatient. At any hour of the day I can hear their cooing love songs. By mid-March, their earliest flimsy nests will be occupied—ready for the first of perhaps three hatchings to come in this year. Several red-winged blackbirds are back in town, exploring fencerows and little cattail wetlands. Their womenfolk will be along later.

On such days as this, when the temperature is a balmy sixty-eight degrees, even the bluebirds are examining the houses scattered here and there around my old weedfields and forest edges. I must go do some obligatory spring cleaning for them. Sap is running strong in the sugar maples, according to a report from the resident yellow-bellied sapsuckers. Clumps of jonquils up and down the lane are reaching for the sun. Catkins on the pussy willows are taking on weight, noticeably.

All this is evidence that would be admissible and considered relevant in any court in the land.

Ready or not, I hereby proclaim spring!

To an Old Farm

This land is now a part of me;
The slope of every ridge
Mirrors the bend of my shoulders.
In spring, pollen of pine
Spices and colors the air
That fills my lungs.

My heart beats
To the roll of thunder,
To the crack of a broken limb
In a December ice storm.
My veins share rainfall
And crystal pond water
With beaver and bluegill,
With heron and dragonfly.

I know its pulse and flow,
The chill of its ice cover,
The balm of its July wash.
Moonlight and starshine,

Sun and long shadows
Bond this land to me,
Delineate my boundaries,
Imprison, and set me free
For surely one more spring.

Illustrations

Fall

Winter

Ora E. Anderson was a journalist, conservationist, naturalist, and artist. He was named honorary lifetime director of the Ohio chapter of The Nature Conservancy and was the recipient of the Ohio Arts Council Governor's Award for the Arts in 1999. He passed away in August 2006 at the age of ninety-four.

Deborah Griffith is managing editor of *Bird Watcher's Digest* and other publications from BWD Press.

Julie Zickefoose, nature artist, writer, and NPR commentator, is the author and illustrator of *Letters from Eden: A Year at Home, in the Woods.*

Jean Andrews is the producer of the video documentary *A Forest Returns: The Success Story of Ohio's Only National Forest as Told by Ora E. Anderson.*